Returning Home
A Travelog in 2012

Returning Home
A Travelog in 2012

Bijoy M Misra
Lincoln, MA, USA

BLACK EAGLE BOOKS

 BLACK EAGLE BOOKS
7464 Wisdom Lane
Dublin, OH 43016
E-mail: info@blackeaglebooks.org
Website: www.blackeaglebooks.org

First published by
BLACK EAGLE BOOKS, 2019

**Returning Home
A Travelog in 2012**

**Bijoy M Misra
Lincoln, MA, USA**
Copyright © Bijoy M Misra

All rights reserved. No part of this publication may be reproduced, stored in a retrieval system, or transmitted, in any form or by any means, electronic, mechanical, photocopying, recording or otherwise without the prior permission of the publisher.

Cover photo: Bijoy M Misra

Cover and Interior Design: Ezy's Publication

Library of Congress Control Number: 2019937802
ISBN-978-1-64560-000-8 (paperback)
ISBN-978-1-64560-001-5 (e-book)

Printed in United States of America

To Shivani, Shalini, Pallavi - my grandchildren. Hopefully it would educate them about the life and society in the ancestral land...

Contents

Foreword	13
Prologue	15
London	19
Arrival	19
Visit to British Museum	22
Delhi	25
Arrival	25
Airport, Taxi Ride	26
Uncle's Apartment	28
Ratha Jatra, Morning Walk, Market Expedition	32
Cousin's House	37
Morning Trip with Uncle	42
Home Shrine, Brigadier's family	48
Departure from Delhi	55
Delhi Airport	57
Flight to Bhubaneswar	60
Orissa	62
Arrival, meeting the sick brother	62
DAY - 1	65
Bhubaneswar	65

Family recollection	65
DAY - 2	72
Chilika	72
Travel to Chilika, Laboratory, Bhagabati Temple	72
Road to Chilika	74
Marine Laboratory	76
Visit to Banapur	78
Chilika Guesthouse	79
DAY - 3	81
Lake, Conference, Forest	81
Tour of Chilika	81
Kalijai Temple	83
Coastal Zone Conference	85
On road to Gulunda	87
Dasapalla, Nayagarh	92
DAY - 4	96
Bhubaneswar	96
Prachi River Valley	96
Reading *Saptasati* in Bhubaneswar	102
DAY - 5	105
Bhubaneswar	105
Wedding Preparation	105
Visit to Sanjoy	108
Visit to Bank	109
Meeting at Technology Park	112
DAY - 6	122
Cuttack Institutions	122

Pre-Wedding Ritual	122
Visit to Uncle's House	125
Visit to High School	128
Saroj, the High School friend	134
Visit to the Vice Chancellor	136
Carnival at Kathjodi	139
D A Y - 7	142
Wedding Event	142
Wedding Preparation	142
Wedding Reception	147
Wedding Ritual	151
D A Y - 8	156
Wedding And Family	156
Post-Wedding Morning Ritual	156
Bhagavadgita reading at Uncle's House	157
Company with the Family Members	163
D A Y - 9	166
Sanskruti Vihar	166
Wedding event conclusion	166
Sanskruti Vihar Club	168
Family Disputes	174
D A Y - 10	178
Jeypore	178
Train Ride to Viziangaram	178
Taxi Travel in the Mountains	186
D A Y - 11	192
Sightseeing At Jeypore	192

Gupteswar Caves	192
Jeypore Wedding Reception	199
Chhattisgarh Waterfalls	201
D A Y - 12	204
Return To Bhubaneswar	204
Borra Caves	204
Road to Visakhapatnam	210
Train to Bhubaneswar	211
D A Y - 13	213
Father's Book Release	213
Address location	213
Purchasing Gifts	215
Book Release Event	217
D A Y - 14	225
Events At Cuttack	225
Upanayana	225
Jâtrâ Danabira Harishchandra	232
D A Y - 15	236
Return To Delhi	236
Departure from Orissa	236
Lunch with Nephew's In-Laws	240
Old College Friends	244
Departure From Delhi	251
Flight to London	251
Night Halt at London	254
Boston	258
Afterword	260
Epilogue	263

India worshipped mothers.
A young woman brought up in a stately family, chose
to camp on the streets following a revolutionary poet.
While the poet felt for the people, the woman felt for
the man, the family, and the people.

Her interest was to visit places with the poet.
The poet valued her, and their son carries her with him.
She is there at every place in this book.
She asked me to write ...

To
the memory of
my father
Manmohan Misra
(1920-2000)

FOREWORD

I enjoy reading travelogues. It is a way to discover and rediscover the diverse world that is our common home and the diverse humanity that is our family. If it is a place that I have already seen or is written about by someone else, a travelogue is a way to know the place through someone else's eyes, someone else's perspective, like taking a second trip. If it is a place that I have never been to, it is an opportunity to discover the place for the first time. I have never been to Orissa so I welcomed the opportunity—thanks to Bijoy Misra—to embark on this travel of discovery through Days in Orissa. It is travel that I shall always remember, always cherish.

Travelogues speak to me in different ways, often through a category. More often they are nostalgic. The writer takes me back to his or her olden days: it is mostly about how things used to be—and with changing times—with a sense of loss. It is an intensely emotional, personal journey—even more, a personal memory. There is much to be said for that, whilst I also have to appreciate it as a journey of the writer—the writer only. Detached from the journey I am a listener.

Then there is the narrative category. The writer describes and documents what comes along the way—what catches the writer's eye, in the way the writer sees it, and what the writer chooses to document. It can be a series of general observations or a chronology of minute details. Maybe it is a place where the writer himself has or has not travelled to before, what the writer sees this time in the way the writer sees it: the writer is my eyes, and it is in the present.

Then there is the holistic category. Yes, there are the nostalgic and narrative elements in it. Those contribute significantly to the richness of the travelogue. But there is more to it, synthesizing philosophical and historical reflections, socio-political awareness, compassionate humanity, and more. Bijoy combines all these without ever losing a sense of travel—with the keen eye of an astute observer, as a participant in dynamic history—through a conscious footing in the present. The personal elements of the travel put a human face to it, at the same time transcending it in a way that is universal. Bijoy has the rare ability to write such a travelogue for Bijoy is a poet, thinker, scientist, and scholar who grew up in Orissa and possesses an intimate knowledge of the region. Could you hope for a better guide than that?

He is a guide at its best—he is a companion who tells you his story, his journey in a way that is fluid, colourful, educative, engaging and inviting. So, join Bijoy on his voyage to Orissa, whether or not you have been there. It will be a memorable travel of discovery—or rediscovery—and your life will be richer. Thanks to Days in Orissa, I feel richer for it.

Sajed Kamal
Boston, Massachusetts.
Two Thousand & Fourteen

PROLOGUE

What is our identity as human beings? Do we have any accountability to the society? To whom are we accountable? We are born into a certain family and at a certain location. For a long time, the family and the family acquaintances nurture us. We develop an attachment to the geographical location of our upbringing. We develop an emotional bond to make us feel at "home" in a setting that lets us meet our friends with whom we had our childhood association. A child has a smaller world retaining most of the experience. Revisiting memory with those with friendly association, we do feel child-like again. Possibly the child in us never grows up. The ado and power we display later are vain and trivial. Living and being happy as a child are the greatest blessings a human being can ask in life!

While growing up in a town called Cuttack in India, I had another aspect to my life not available to many. My father would hide in low thatched huts in paddy fields a few miles from our home and I would have to struggle to figure a face inside that overflowing beard. Little did I know that this was a sacrifice people made in order to build a nation such that the fellow humans may get their rights protected. My mother, dainty as she was, was right in the ally in this drama. Meetings would happen, flowers would be thrown, songs would be sung, and my father would be home for a few weeks until the next episode would begin. I am not sure who controlled these episodes, and why my father was volunteering for this adventure. I never asked. All in the family and all in the neighbourhood loved him, and I loved him too. Not many in similar situations had a family or a son. A son to my father was my identity.

When I learned to read, and could read newspapers, I learned that I had certain rights by virtue of the language I spoke. I would accompany my mother, or sometimes an uncle, to the sand bed of the local Kathjodi[1] River to hear some of the most articulate orations made in my language Oriya. I loved the fluency; I loved the sincerity of the speakers. Good language is nectar to a young person of seven years of age. I saw that with my children, I see that with my granddaughters who are crossing that age. Language arouses curiosity; it creates imagination. Seven is the connecting age to the universe. The sonority of the oration however would not bring father to dinner at home, but would take him to a jail cell somewhere. The boy's life gets confused with a missing father. Meetings would continue; others would speak; protests would proliferate until someone would die through a police gun shot. These were rebellion days in the new-born democracy; each

---

[1] *It is a branch of the River Mahanadi flowing to the south of Cuttack.*

group asserting identity, asking for security. It was not clear if people volunteered to die, or the police killed the innocent. Sacrifices occasionally bring results; Orissa and Oriyas had to fight for their demands through such agitations.

This formed my identity as a human being. Then I had the added responsibility of what I do with it. Did it help me or hurt me? Did I have a choice? Should I not feel happy at a place that accepted me? Why should I go anywhere else? Was it to feed myself or to evaluate my identity? Must I compete in the world to win, or, must I feel happy to survive? Did I exploit my identity to gain, or, did I nurture it to cherish? Did I have a duty towards the people who gave me my identity? Did I have a duty for those individuals who died in helping to create my identity? Questions come, but I always suppressed them. Life does not allow us to ask or answer questions. Many times, we pretend not to know them. Life creates situations and does not give us enough time or intelligence to sort them out. Often, we get tired and die before having an opportunity to look back at life. Many times, life looks ugly and we try to forget the past. Rarely, we gather courage to observe our traced path and check what is left. By the time, we think of our teachers, most are dead. The design of the universe is not one of gratitude but one of survival. A slight instability, and you can lose your ground! Most look at the ground immediately below and possibly five feet around. To look at a tree is a rare privilege indeed!

If you keep a thought in mind, opportunity may show up. So was the summer of 2012. I lost my father in 2000 and my mother in 2009. I had to observe my personal family to determine if they forgave me for my less than adequate availability over the years. I had to gather the spiritual energy to look back at the boy of seven in those Kathjodi sands. I had to extrapolate the enthusiasm that created my identity some fifty- eight years ago. I had to meet hundreds of my brothers, sisters and friends. I had to connect my world to theirs. I had seen it before, but always constrained with the issues of the family and the problems associated with them. Most orators from the Kathjodi sands have disappeared or live the last days somewhere in quiet. We celebrate my father locally to claim that we did not forget. We do not have the courage or the resources to bring all our people together. We think somebody else would do, nobody does. First time ever I visit with unconstrained open eyes. I want to see, visit, hug, sing and dance. I want to become a boy of seven. I begin my journey on a Virgin Atlantic flight from Boston on route to London. This was eighteenth of June, 2012.

LONDON
Arrival

I reached London 19th June morning, 7 AM. London Heathrow Airport is like a zoo with a maze of alleys, subways, stairs, "do-not-enter" signs. Pathways wind miles before anything interesting may happen. The interesting thing that happens is someone shouting to advise to stay in lane, or directing to go in a different lane. A few brown-skinned western attired individuals with airport badges walk around trying to keep order in the enormous traffic. The traffic converges from all parts of the planet; some look like coming from the Mars! Attires, hairdos, ornaments, men in tunics, women in cloaks; colourful and strange - Heathrow is a sight to behold! Amidst these could be the potential terrorists, a confused group of travellers lurking to cause harm! London has witnessed terrorist acts before. It was alert in the morning. Olympics were coming soon. The city was trying its best to be a good host.

We all landed up in an enormous hall. There were two lanes now; one for people who belonged to the European Union; and the other for everyone else. I saw a third lane at the end labelled "Fast Track." Since I would be in London only until the evening, I thought that lane could be good for me. I asked an Officer. He saw my US passport and directed me to the longest line, the second one. I was now the last after several hundred tired individuals. Lines moved in the slowest pace. Suddenly a massive Chinese group showed up and advanced to the front. The athletes have priority! The Chinese had shown up to acclimatize themselves to London weather. Money does create opportunity! The group made various noises expressing confusion, but it did get quiet after a couple of officials showed up. They helped diffuse the commotion.

To observe people waiting in line at airports is an interesting experience. Some look tense, some look resigned; some others give a gleeful "it is the way" look. Most women smile if you exchange glance with them. Elderly and youthful men nod head. Ethnic men look away "none of your business" type. The strangely dressed men, who could be kings in some island clan, give a look of despair. They are certainly used to better service in their fiefdom. Most interesting are men with multiple women towing along. It did not occur to me that the women could be the assembly of the man's multiple wives. I had made friends with an elderly group from New Zealand. They were returning from a "spiritual mission" to India. Many such groups from Australia and New Zealand do humanitarian work in the hill areas in India and hunt for potential finds to convert to Christianity. They appear jolly. They think they rescue people from poverty, which they apparently do. But they manage to take away the person's identity! The person succumbs to food and goods! There is tension of "Christian conversion" in India.

I cleared myself out of the jungle and went through the Customs. Then I came to another large open space that happens in all airports. In Boston, they have made the space friendly with recessed lighting, high ceilings and wall sculptures. In London, it was neon and concrete. It was another zoo. I noticed my nephew Sandeep who had relocated to London. He is part of a new import from India to the advanced countries as a trade in the electronic age. With the amount of exports, one would think that India might have reached high edge in electronics, but that was not the case. Indian boys and girls seem to have aptitude for logic and numbers. Work in computers was a Godsend to India's employment problem. It was a new kind of business. There were many tiers of brokers involved; Romney's model to make money sitting in Cayman Islands! India had entered the power game of modern capitalism. Middlemen made money by trading talents. It was a "no-investment" business!

We took a cab and reached my nephew's apartment after a ninety-minute ride. I met his wife. She was also a computer professional. They had a three-month old son. To be a young person of Indian origin is a blessing and curse together. It is a blessing because of the enormous affection that is germane in Indian society. And it is a curse because the system lacks the opportunities to train oneself in school. While such a young person carries better manners than many, the individual could remain limited in thinking and constrained in scope. The British engineered education system in India to create clerk assistants to help in their administration. The system is still active. India continued to be in the shadows of the old colony. I managed to survive in the system and veered to the sciences. The young men and women of India were gradually getting separated from her rich culture without getting into a good grounding in the languages and literature. Countries do get destroyed by occupation. India's recovery could take a few centuries more. It was in a survival mode now. There was happiness if one made a decent living. It was a technical way to subdue human aspiration. There was little connection to the thinking and creative pursuits that made India the envy of the world. The young people live in the present. They have no choice; they lack good teachers, sincere mentors. Some religious preachers tout as teachers to make business. The good news is that some young people maintained their sanity against the huge odds. My nephew was one of them. I loved the way this young family was approaching life. They had aspiration.

Visit to British Museum

I took a shower and we had a quick lunch. Sandeep had taken the day off to accompany me to the British Museum in which I had my personal interest to learn about the artefacts from India. We took a train and reached the Museum at about 1 PM. It was a massive place. Buildings were constructed in some arbitrary way around a colossal courtyard. The entrances to the buildings appeared disconnected. The British culture does like the maze style discoveries. Tour guides were escorting various foreign groups. Guide in a Museum is a good profession to help find your way in the jungle of numbered buildings. We arrived at the South Asia section and I was pleased with the display. There were exquisite carvings, beautifully made metal and ivory objects. There were broken religious artefacts from the temple walls. Some complete stone structures were reassembled on site. I wondered why people took time to lift items from another country, but I marvelled at the beauty and the grandeur of the display. I had told my children when they were small that people of Indian descent could be generically artistic in nature. I looked at my hands and did not think I would have the patience to create any of the objects I saw in display. Indians think art as a God's gift. I was curious why God allowed such gifts to be stolen!

I saw a large collection of objects from Orissa, the area of my origin. Many of the objects might have been stolen from myriads of unguarded temples in our land. Stone carving flourished in Orissa beginning with the caves in pre-Christian days. Mammoth temples were built with exquisite artwork and masonry. The whole history of the technology and the production has not been compiled. The artisans did move to South East Asia to help build colossal works there. Orissa also produced the magnificent palm-leaf manuscripts decorated with art work. The early religious scholars of Jainism and Buddhism had the fancy of recording their sermons in palm leaf "books." The older tradition what we call Hindus preferred the sound retention through oral communication. The Hindu books came to be recorded much late. Orissa is the store house of massive collections of palm-leaf manuscripts waiting to be compiled and deciphered.

I was pleased to view the collection from my area. The jewellery section was gorgeous. Metal architecture through heat and compression is still a traditional art in Orissa. The objects had curatorial legends, which I thought needed more research. I saw beautiful hard wood door panels, spears, axes, and other prehistoric artefacts. I learned about my history. The Englishmen had kept a memory of my country in their land; my forefathers were their subjects.

Time was limited. The Museum closed at 5 PM. We walked to Covent Garden nearby to wait for another nephew of mine who works as an officer in a Bank. Because of his responsibility in work, he could not take time off and could only see us after work. His father is the younger brother to me and has been sick with a traumatic head injury for a couple of years now. My nephew took care of him with diligence and patience through visits and resources. Sandeep and I camped ourselves in a rustic looking food place. We ordered juice and sandwich. The second nephew Kirti showed up and we three felt at home in the company. Kirti is poised, he is a serious individual. We chatted on life, society, people, India and England; we shared views. I listened to them and enjoyed their discourse. They were the new youth of India. They were aware of their glorious heritage but had little access. Making a living had made them new slaves to the moneyed individuals. Their creativity had little scope to blossom. I wondered if this was how civilizations died.

    Kirti volunteered to escort me to the airport. I had to take the flight to Delhi in the night. We took the train and reached the airport at 9 PM. Now, it was my time with the maze towards the gate! I went through the security check which was unusually swift. I proceeded to the gate to take the flight at 10:30 PM.

DELHI
Arrival

Here I was headed to the country of my origin. Landing in India always brings ecstasy and nostalgia. While flying over Pakistan, there is a thought of looking down the troubled piece of the world. There is an air of affinity when one lands in India. It is a mixed feeling of happiness in meeting friends and acquaintances along with the knowledge of the bereavements and misery. It is an adventure to witness the survival struggle of the millions!

I have lived in the US for about forty years. There was a feel of jubilation as the aircraft touched the land. Sometimes there is expressed jubilation by the passengers to exhibit the happiness that they survived the flight safely. An immigrant's jubilation is different. One misses the sights and sounds of home when one lives abroad. The food though cooked with the right recipe could taste different. The dress might not fit. India on the other hand has a pull. The average Indian is friendly. Indians are welcoming and hospitable. You can trust the person for help. People would go out of their way to help a stranger. The old India had declared that "let the guest be treated like a god!"

Airport, Taxi Ride

India time was 11 AM in the morning. Unlike the reception halls abroad, the arrival hall in India normally has dim lights and would look messy. This time it was tidy - the floor was clean, the wall had a fresh coat of paint. Particularly the lighting was good. I noticed that India was emerging from her days of neglect and was trying to get attention in the free world. The officers were better dressed, the lines moved well. There were two lines: one for people with Indian passports and another for everyone else. The duty-men had heckled me a couple times during my earlier visits while I went through the Indian passport line. The stamp of my new nationality protected me in my country of origin! When I arrived at the desk officer, he asked how long I might stay. My answer of two and half weeks satisfied him. I was out to pick up my luggage and go through the Customs. Nobody looked at me in the Customs. I was suddenly out in a cavernous space. The space was immense; it could invite people without homes to live there! I bought a prepaid taxi coupon. Then I ordered a cup of coffee.

My uncle lived in Delhi. After working as an Electrical engineer in various paper mills in India, he retired as the Chairman of the autonomous Hindustan Paper Corporation. I loved him; he used to bring me special sweets when I was a kid. He had a liking towards me. I was the best boy in his wedding. It was the sixtieth anniversary of his wedding. He had turned 85 and my aunt was 75. I see them once in five years or so. This time I was making special effort to spend some time with them. Both my parents had passed away. We need an elder to discuss life. I was in search of such an elder. I had arranged with my friends in Delhi to host a sixtieth anniversary event for the couple. The event was not going to happen for many reasons. I had been curious.

I loaded my luggage on a cart and left the hall. Suddenly a flash of raw heat struck me. Sometimes my body might handle the heat; my eyes do not. They dry up causing me enormous discomfort. I faced the devil and moved forward to my taxi. Two boys drove up in a box like object to the spot number sixteen. One of the boys picked up my bag. He declared that the bag was heavy and said it would cost ten rupees extra. I smiled to myself. Having stayed overseas for a long time one did not relate to the affection to the rupees. I thought that the boy's work was easily two hundred rupees. I did not open my mouth. Heat does not allow you to utter words; you just keep going. The taxi did start; it moved. The inside looked like Uncle Tom's cabin with a beaten-up décor. I tried to close the window, but it would not. Then I tried to get attention of the boys. They were too busy in some serious conversation. I was a confined object in a cage. I tried to protect myself from the gusts of heat. It was not succeeding.

A taxi ride in a major Indian city is an acrobatic experience. Everything is a circus act in high ropes; all look orchestrated. There is an element of danger all around but fortunately nobody dies under your watch. It is a necessary feat for all riders in India, but the length of the journey can provoke intimidation. Mine was long. I wanted to understand the traffic; why they stopped and moved; what moved and how close could my box go to the other box! Everything was grazing ballistics; came close, did not hit, like asteroids approaching earth every second. In a traffic halt lasting several minutes, I did speak to the driver of my thought of picking some fruits if possible. He agreed. He then jettisoned to another inter-planetary journey. In the near earth orbits the debris is enormous; it needs special skills to manoeuvre. I remained happily caged. There was danger outside. However fragile the cage might be, there was a boundary!

I did have some vague idea of where my uncle lived. It started looking a bit familiar. While I was thinking to myself that I must forget the fruits, the box stopped near a pushcart selling watermelons. I bought a watermelon and some lichee[2]. I told the vendor that I needed mangoes. He asked if I would need a box. I nodded and asked where it was. He told that it would come in a minute. A boy suddenly jumped the road amidst the rolling traffic and picked up a box from the other side! A little Hanuman in action! I paid the bill and there was gratitude.

Now I had the difficult task of finding the building that my uncle lived. All buildings looked alike and there were no street signs. I gave the driver the telephone number and he called to get the directions. From the conversation, I heard left, right, left etc. I remained unsettled. Against my weak confidence, things did happen. Hoila! we arrived in front of my uncle's apartment building. The guard opened the door as a courtesy and we drove in. Now I discovered that my driver's companion had disappeared. I tried to recall where the separation happened, I did not have a clue. The driver helped to take my suitcase up the elevator. We were in front of another location with B Misra sign on the door. I felt delighted. I pressed the bell.

Uncle's Apartment

My uncle opened the door. I touched his feet and offered my respects. He looked shorter than I had imagined.

---

[2] *A tropical fruit popular in South Asia.*

We shrink as we age. He looked reduced. I rolled my luggage in. I did not feel tired, but I was in a different time cycle, possibly I needed a good shower. There were thick drapes over the backside glass doors. An air conditioner sat on another window. It was going full blast. There were three fans spinning on the ceiling. Uncle said to cool down a bit since electricity could go away in the afternoon. My aunt showed up from the other room. She is nice and polished. She is always with her smile and an affectionate look. I hugged her. She offered me water to drink.

The "uncle" is an institution in human life. I had just been an uncle in London. As an uncle one can act like a father, but need not be responsible like a father. One can confer with an uncle as a friend; he would find time for you. Fathers are too busy; they ignore that special time children seek when growing up. It is not clear if this is by design. It prevails among the animals. An uncle walks with you, jokes with you and treats you as an equal. Fathers love you, support you, but you know that all cannot be told. Mothers are your conduit to fathers on difficult matters. An uncle is mother and father combined; nothing is difficult. He can ask and you are obliged to be candid. There is mutual respect. There is no higher or lower; your good conduct is rewarded plenty.

Uncle guided me to a room I had used before. It had a nice bedspread; it looked colourful. There was a small shrine in front, a dressing table on the side. There was an air conditioner humming at the window insulating us from the sizzling heat outside. I wondered if the acrobatic traffic slowed down in the heat, it was different inside. After a wash, up and a shower, we sat down for lunch. After two hundred years of British in India, India was a semi-western country. The city dwellers did not practice the multipurpose use of space as happened in the villages. There were special dining areas with furniture sometimes used for study as I did during my city living as a kid. I had loved the free uncluttered flow of space in the village where an entire village could come and sit on the floor. The Japanese still do it. The British had the goal of dividing India into smaller units. Abroad people live in their individual holes. People call it privacy!

My aunt is a good cook. Food was simple, some fish there along with lentils and rice. She said that the fish was fresh; I tried a bit. The food was tasty. Rice in India is different from the rice abroad. I liked the crystal nature of the grains. She opened the mango box and the mangoes looked green. I felt bad that I did not check inside the box. The fruit vendor had said that this variety did not change the outside colour. The inside had a beautiful orange red hue, I loved the contrast with the green top. I took a piece and it was the sweetest thing on earth! India was my home; I should spend the summer there for the mangoes. Uncle did not take any piece, I was puzzled. I thought to myself that some old age disease possibly had crept in to prevent him to consume fructose. My aunt intervened saying that he only took mango in a milk shake! I wished I had grown up in colonial days. I admired my aunt to continue to support these odd luxuries of my uncle. She might have her own food luxuries I would not know. My mother had. It was 2:30 now; we retired to our rooms. I was fast asleep in a couple of minutes.

The clock said 4 PM. A little sleep is always refreshing; the afternoon sleep after a sleep-deprived night is lovely. I sprang up, everything looked brighter. Looking at objects is a state of the mind. I saw more, I noticed more. I could gauge the age of the air-conditioner and noticed the grain of the dressing table panels. I noticed my own clumsiness of my scattered objects and papers, I arranged them to order. I could feel the light of the sun peeping through the drapes. It felt like morning, it could be. My body clock was ten hours behind.

I came out of the room to the dining area and uncle was already making tea. We sat down to the fine aroma of the Indian tea, a luxury for me rarely achieved. I love the taste and the flavour, it is just right. I looked for aunt, and learned that she had slipped away to her afternoon Bridge group. I had heard of the group in my earlier trips. I admire the women to bond together. Indian women are strong and bright. Sita had her way to do things she thought right. The society demands education for gainful employment. Family and economic situations deprive most women of a formal education, some limp up to High School. While motherhood and home-management are great activities, the women can have more gainful living. In my younger days, I had visited villages in Andhra Pradesh where illiterate women would proudly display their alphabet writing on slates. Women are pragmatic and they take everything on stride. An Indian woman takes pride being a mother. Such an attribute is possibly universal, but not always as candid as displayed in India.

Uncle and I talked. This was the first time I was talking to someone high in the family after my mother passed away three years ago. I looked at him to advise me what role I might have to keep the family and children together. He told me about his own loneliness and attachment to his children. Now since he had aged he does not feel confident in traveling long distances. Aunt did not allow him to drive; so, he had the only option of walking in the neighbourhood. His two daughters lived in Delhi. They showed up every week. They taught in the local schools. The youngest child lived in Australia, and was a CPA. We talked about family and people in it. The family was large. My uncle had great admiration to my father and it showed in everything he said. Between them, they had three sisters; uncle was indifferent towards them. All of them had passed away. The sisters adored my father and he loved them. Human attitude is subjective. Forgiveness possibly works, but does not manifest easily.

Deepa, uncle's older daughter, and her husband showed up in the evening with their daughter. The daughter had recently married and would be flying to the US in two weeks. I like Deepa very much. She is kind and affectionate. I wanted to discuss the sixtieth anniversary event. My uncle was not enthusiastic. The younger daughter Seema lost her husband a few months back. The customs demanded that the family went mourning for a year. I did see the merit of a person of eighty-five years celebrating an event though other happened around. He had a different viewpoint. We came from a conservative heritage. My opinion did not count, but I am not convinced. India lived through her customs. I had to yield!

Ratha Jatra, Morning Walk, Market Expedition

The day was June 21, the Ratha Jatra[3] day in Puri. I had timed my trip to be in Delhi by the Ratha Jatra day to witness the festival at the local temple in Hauz Khas. Having spent my early years in our village, I had special fascination to the Temple and the deity. My grandmother was an

---

[3] *Known as Car Festival, an annual ritual that collects millions of pilgrims to Puri, India. The ritual could be Buddhist in origin. It is currently celebrated as the outing of the deities in Sri Jagannatha Temple in Puri.*

ardent devotee. She could convince us that the deity was a living object. After being abroad, I had visited ISKON temples in various cities to get a glimpse of the deity. Lately I had learned Sanskrit to recite the prayers. Twenty years ago, I helped install the deities at the Temple in Nashville. I visited every year religiously until the death of my father. I took a break. Here in Delhi, I had timed it such that the nephew could be with his uncle and aunt to receive the special blessings from the Lord.

The Hauz Khas Temple was special to me. I had been there whenever an opportunity arose. Last time I was there in 1999 when I wanted to pray for my father's health. I had been in Orissa to help in the Cyclone Relief and after ten days of intense travel, I happened to witness strange symptoms of a disease in my father that was incapacitating his memory. I told my mother that I would stay with him. She advised that I must do what I came for and father was appreciating what I was doing. She said that my engagement in the relief work kept him happy. Father himself did not know that he was sick. He had developed acute dementia. He knew that people were suffering. He would glue himself to the TV. I did not know that was a symptom. The doctors said there was no cure. I felt bad; lost. The doctors showed me the MRIs that the brain was shrinking. It was unsettling. I was not prepared to deal with the health issues with my father. It did not come up before!

Father's life had been strange. His father worked as the Police Chief in the kingdom of Baudh[4] in Orissa. Father

---

[4] *A former princely state in western Orissa, currently made into an administrative district.*

was born there. In the late 20's, the King of Baudh tried to punish some people by bringing the British Regent from Ranchi. This was against my grandfather's conscience. The entire family packed their luggage on a few horses and left the kingdom in the dead of the night. Once you are the Police Chief you possibly can travel freely in the night! They returned to their ancestral place near Puri to restart life. Grandfather thought that Lord Jagannatha helped him in the escape. My father turned out to be a good student and became a prolific orator. While in college, he spoke in public rally at Puri and received a jail sentence. This was 1936; he was a sixteen-year-old boy. Detentions and jails followed him the rest of his life. He expressed his mind all his life. He said there needed to be a voice to speak on behalf of the common man! He lived his life to experience the misery of the toiling public.

In Delhi, we were to our beautiful cup of aromatic tea. Kakei (We call Kakei and Khudi for uncle and aunt in our home) asked if I would give company in his morning walk. I wilfully agreed. We drove up a short distance to a parking area and then entered an urban oasis. Kakei told me that it was a thirty-acre park. Some of his friends were already returning from their walk. They were asking why my uncle did not show up earlier. Apparently, he missed the previous day also. Friends have a right to imagine things when you do not show up. This gets more traction when one gets old. Ageing is the greatest insecurity in the world! I loved the care that my uncle's friends showed. Old friends have a charm. My father was too public. People expected things get done through him. He did not have a safety net besides my mother. I wondered which way I would go when I would be older!

We proceeded further and I heard more "misraji"[5] calls. I loved those affectionate vocatives. Kakei and I reached a place where there were a few benches and some people were sitting. Kakei said it was their discussion group. Kakei introduced me and I joined their discussion. The whole world was on discourse including their own. I was seeing a mini India, one moved without visiting places. Some women and young girls walked by. The trail could be cleaner, but it was fair. The trees looked dull; all were waiting for the rains. In the distance, a few people were doing yoga exercises. On another bench, a man was sitting in a meditative pose. Practicing meditation amongst the traffic of human beings is an achievement only Indians can create!

We returned. It was a relaxing experience. Kakei turned on the TV and there was the view from Puri. I did not know that there was a full day broadcast from Puri. The view was nostalgic. I had been there. I had touched the chariot and the deities. We would plant ourselves in choice locations and would have the balcony view of the procession. The whole process was celebratory. It is supposed to be a faith celebration. I am unsure if the faith is internal or external. I think faith is imagination. I admire the artist who created the stunning iconography. The size, the shape, and the angle of view are just right. Such an object cannot have hands or legs. It is artistic, it is not an after-thought. Some commentators were shouting that it was the depiction of a shapeless Brahman; they forgot that it was a human imagination of an artistic beauty. A "shapeless" object has no "shape!" An artist sees inside. The Vedas call him *kavi*, the poet.

---

[5] *"ji" is added as a respectful vocative to the name.*

Commentaries continued, they did not have much substance. Things have changed little in forty years since I heard these last. I found the oratory less fluent, the recitations less spontaneous. I did not check who the people were. They were trying hard, but the language was not elegant as in the past. I did not know what audience they were looking for. Possibly the effort was to get something going with the video. The video was excellent; the technology was working. Kakei and I watched it. Khudi watched Wimbledon Tennis in the other room. She was a sports fan. She knew the game; she knew the players. She had her favourites. She did not shout as I did while watching a game!

I took a shower and we had breakfast. I checked the feasibility of going to Hauz Khas. I did not want to push Kakei to come; but I had no independence of traveling alone in Delhi. It was possibly another atrocious day waiting outside. A friend of mine had given me a mobile phone and I could put some money to it to make contacts with people. Khudi volunteered to go with me and we went out on a marketing trip.

In case you happen to go into the side lanes in Delhi for marketing, you must keep a good eye on your steps. It is not that the road would be uneven; occasionally it may not exist! There could be huge drops waiting to happen unexpectedly. Drops can be of dissimilar height and hence the best and only solution is to watch your step all the time. To look for a store and to watch your step needs excellent eye and foot coordination! The sharpness needs to be exponential if there is a water or food spill. The trouble we found was that the phone stores did not service every phone. The directions were again like "left, right and next to." To find and negotiate the location of the "next to" needed another mental skill. After bumping over a few places, we reached a store that could help. The person at the counter asked me the number of my telephone. I had no clue. While I felt embarrassed, the store person said she could find out. Now she did a multi-phone Mars relay and told me my number. I paid her money and the funds were transacted electronically. We retraced our path, the time with a little more confidence. I watched my step. We negotiate heights better than the falls!

On our way, back, we stopped by at a vegetable vendor. He had a few items scattered here and there. They did not look too interesting. It seemed vegetables came every morning and they dry out quickly. The vendor did not make a mess with water. Khudi bought some stuff; half a bag vegetables came to a hundred rupees. I thought that was expensive. Kakei had told us to get some flowers. We stopped by at a flower vendor and picked up some flowers. We were on our last leg of the trek back to the apartments. Khudi entered a gate that said "No Entry". I followed. We oozed out the other side in front of our building. Delhiwallas know their way; others only follow!

Cousin's House

The chariots had started moving. Kakei liked the commotion conveyed through the visual. People were trying to ride up the chariots. There were police around and they were free to beat up the pilgrims in the heat of action. I have never figured out what motivates a person to be a policeman. Beating appears as a natural attribute to police. In some places, they don't mind killing in the name of self-protection! But they also keep the communities safe and occasionally sacrifice themselves!

I tried to reach the widow of my cousin on her mobile

phone. She was from the Sikh community and was a mother. I did not know why my cousin came to live in Delhi. He had become a successful home tutor. His father was my mother's younger brother and was a good teacher. He taught me language in Middle School. Tutoring to do good in competitive examinations was a good business; but the competition had increased. My nephew tutored children of people in business houses and gained a reputation. Uncle Bira, called Biramamu[6], did pass away at an age that I have crossed now. They belonged to the extended Kar family in Cuttack district. Long time ago their predecessors ruled Orissa. They maintained the style, but lost their property after the land reforms enactment in 1951. Highly literary and patriotic, they lived noble ideals in service. My cousin used to help me out during my prior trips to Delhi. He himself passed away in a massive stroke three years ago. He had not even turned forty years of age.

Ritu calls me Bhaina as Jitu did. Her "bha" is different, it sounds distorted. To apply aspiration on a stop sound is not easy for many. We develop accent through our mothers. We carry our labels in the world through our accent. Ritu is from Punjab. Lately most children go to the English-speaking schools and the new breed is increasing. They are heaping themselves up to maintain the foreign call-centres, a good place to hide to make an income. The future of the breed is unknown. English was planted by the British to erase Indian culture from India!

Ritu's words were affectionate. I had thought that I would go to visit her from Hauz Khas, but the plans on the ground were different. She had said that her parents and her brother have moved over to live with her. I wanted

---

[6]*mâmu is the Oriya name for a maternal uncle.*

to meet her parents and offer my condolence. She worked in an office. I learned that her grandfather had passed away the previous week and everyone had gone to village. She would be going to join the family after the office closed Friday. Her brother would accompany her.

She insisted that I visit her. She did not know my insecurity in Delhi travel. She suggested that I take an auto-rickshaw to the "Institutional Area" where she could meet me after the offices closed at 5 PM. I had little information to figure out what this "Institutional Area" was. I went on to think what institutions might exist. I was convinced it was another maze. She confidently gave me another marker, Aruna Asaf Ali Marg.

Kakei, Khudi and I took lunch; I was picturing Ritu as a widow. I had seen her when my cousin first started dating her. That was 1998. Biramâmuhad passed away the previous year. I had forgotten that Jitu had taken me as the elder in the family. His place in Delhi was a mini hostel. Anyone with slightest connection to Orissa had a place there. Objects belonging to various people would be stored all over. Oriyas help each other and Jitu excelled in the art. My first advice to Jitu was to reduce his gestures in hospitality in case he wanted a bride. Our hearts are big, but we load it on our wives! Jitu had told me that he loved Ritu because she liked people; that she enjoyed cooking for them. Here I was; she wanted to offer hospitality even though Jitu had finished his play abruptly three years ago!

I contemplated on my impending expedition. What I would need is a good auto driver who could read sincerity in me. I would reward him, but he should be friendly to me. Another year I had hired an auto to the Chandini Chowk area to buy sweets, it was rough! Human beings live with their memory. Memory gives education, teaches defence. I am past sixty and have gained some experience. The way to reduce commotion is to be prepared and to be alert. Escaping commotion is superior to shouting; shouting is a two- way process. I gained confidence to hit the road. I thought of a few friends whom I could summon in case I am stuck. I carried my mobile communication device with me. It was working.

At 4 PM, I put on my shoes and walked towards the road. I picked up an auto where the driver looked trustworthy. I said my destination; he said "seventy rupees". I had nothing to argue, I thought the task was done. We proceeded. After some time, we stopped at a massive overpass. Nothing moved; the driver stopped the engine. I was determined not to express my insecurity. Internally I was puzzled. After ten minutes or so that felt like years, the impasse ended. After several more of 'stop and go's I suddenly saw the sign of Aruna Asaf Ali Marg. I was delighted. The auto had turned in the right direction. I telephoned Ritu. I told her my location on the road and she said that I should just wait there. There was victory in the first lap. I disposed of the auto and waited on the sidewalk. In a few minutes, I saw a tall personable woman briskly pacing towards my direction. I admired her grace and majesty. I recognized her. Women indeed are a work of art!

Ritu suggested if we should try the subway. Jitu had shown me the subway construction. Instead of digging down as mostly done in the west, here it went overhead. Digging down would have uncovered good archaeology, but would have required displacing many people. Delhi's history remains buried. Compared to London or New York, Delhi is older. We rode the subway. It was nice and clean. The best of all, it was air-conditioned. We got down at Sultanpur and we got into an auto. Jitu's building had a house number; I had no idea where the counting began. The way we reached was not linear. I remain confounded with the number logic that marked houses in Indian cities. In India, counting is an art. It is a combination of Hindu, Greek, Islam and British – all in a lucky Powerball.

We climbed the stairs to the fourth floor. I entered a nicely kept room. I loved the simplicity and the orderliness. Ritu's brother showed up and he escorted me to a room that had an air-conditioner. The brother worked in a school; the family had a taxi business. Ritu and I talked about Jitu, life and Delhi. I had helped Jitu to offload some of the loan towards the house. The adjustable interest rate had increased and mortgage instalment had become high. It is a two-bedroom unit. It has appreciated quite a bit because of the proximity to the subway. Between the brother and sister, they managed home; the little girl went to a private school in the city. Expenses did add up.

After supper, Ritu's brother Rob offered to drop me off in Kakei's place. That relieved me of the biggest burden for the evening. He gave me a helmet to put on. Brother said his turban passed as his own helmet. I rode in the back of his motorbike. In the evening coolness, the electric speed of the bike was a new experience. We jumped barriers, lights, objects and animals. Occasionally Rob would summon me to learn about the affairs at back. I would express my insecure confidence though a feeble voice. Audible or inaudible, the journey would resume as a dolphin striding in the ocean. Time had come to ask if we were on the right road. After taking directions, we had another rocket journey until we came to a dark road that was supposed to lead to Kakei's place. Nothing looked familiar; there was no road mark. I should feel scared at 11

PM, but I was expected to be in safe hands. Someone said we had to go further. After a mile or so, I saw the sign of Don Bosco High School. I was now used to these transitions of fear, wonder, amazement and relief. I guided Rob to Kakei's complex. He wanted to return home. We bade good-bye. I thought about that mystery man who biked with loud noise near our house in the US every morning. Travel with noise possibly gives a feel of accomplishment. Quietness is the ground state for the humans, Bharata wrote in Natyashastra. I walked quietly inside the building.

Morning Trip with Uncle

The date was Friday, June 22. Fridays were special for me for a while. While returning from India in one of such trips in the '80s, my mother had made a parting statement that some astrologer had told her that she might not survive more than ten months. To me this was the most mischievous forecast ever made by any person. Some god-men breeding trust through dress have a habit of communicating such profound-sounding prognostication in a soft voice. People in vulnerable situations have no other choice than believing them. I had little response except saying that I would pray hard on her behalf. I had shaky confidence that things should be all right though I was puzzled.

Returning to the US, the alleged forecast remained as a serpent on my neck. I went on looking for a possible recourse that might "neutralize" the prognostication. The local temple priest suggested *Devî*[7] worship every Friday

---

[7] *The Sanskrit name for a universal mother, manifesting as the regulator of the living forces in the universe. Hindus believe that the activities are the play of the Devî.*

evening. I tried to undertake the task. I brushed my Sanskrit and read the crisp *Devi* poetry every Friday for two hours. I did not have the courage to check with my mother to get any new predictions. On phone calls, she would not bring it up. The matter died without further hitch though the Devi reading stayed with me as a new task in life. I do resort to it when I feel the need. Lately I have tried to gain some understanding of the conceptual power in *Devi* cosmology. My admiration for the Indian poets and thinkers has increased because of it. It is a humble logic to think of a Universal Mother nurturing us. Why not? What else?

Morning 6 AM was special in Kakei's home. He would make the fragrant tea with his engineering precision; then he would add milk to create a brand colour. The hot decoction would then be poured into a thermos flask and the flask would stand in royal uprightness on the dining table. Two flat bottom teacups would be laid out on two perpendicularly placed place mats. A box of cookies and another container of other snacks would alight from the side shelf. The tea ceremony would begin. Kakei would pour tea into the cups. He would ask me to add sugar, which I would do. I admired the setting, the dignity. Indian snacks are special. Tea with dry hot snacks is extra-special. They do not make such hot snacks elsewhere in the world. I wonder if anyone created a recipe for the event. The ritual could have a multi-culture origin.

We went for our walk to the park. We arrived straight at the meeting site. Kakei's friends asked me how my time had been. I expressed my gratitude. I sought counsel on the proper etiquette to meet a Brigadier's widow, who had lost her only son recently. An elderly Bengali person with only a few teeth in his mouth burst out. He said that he came from a military family. He said his father beat him bad when he was fifteen. He ran away from home. He became an engineer through his own efforts. He never looked back. He did not know if any in his family was alive. The man looked dignified with his old age. He spoke easily. I was witnessing a different India. Nobody asked him anything, I did not pursue further. His story was irrelevant to my question. My question had died. There was some other discussion on corruption charges against the government. There were various opinions. Kakei did not participate. The meeting ended. Kakei and I returned.

Back in the car, Kakei asked me if he could show me around Delhi a bit. I agreed and we went ahead. He knew his way around and we arrived at the Bahai temple site, the beautiful sculpture designed as a full-blossomed lotus flower. A sign said that the gates would open at 10 AM. We were disappointed. Kakei then continued the journey and we reached the Delhi Kali temple. Possibly, he had gauged my Friday connection to *Devi*. The Temple had two dozen steps to climb. Kakei stayed downstairs; climbing steps was not comfortable to his ankles. He advised me to go up and take a tour and I did. On our return journey, he showed me various buildings and new construction. We seemed to have gotten lost since we were on a never-ending road with no traffic lights. We recovered and reached back home. Kakei was proud of his cognitive skills that he tested. I felt foolish, I did not notice the test.

At home, I had fruits and cereals for breakfast. We sat with the newspapers in the comfortable sitting area. I thought of making a few phone calls in planning the rest part of my journey. I also thought of my wife and home back in the US. It was not easy to find a reasonable window of time to call the US from India. Indian service providers worked perpetual night shifts to hit the daylight in the US. I did not know if they enjoyed it. I settled for sending an email and calling home early morning the next day to get to the US in the night.

Pradeep had dropped off my air ticket to Bhubaneswar at Kakei's house. Pradeep was Jitu's brother and worked as a lawyer in the Delhi Bar. He had advised me that the air ticket paid through Indian currency could cost less than paying through foreign currency. He had proceeded to buy the ticket and I would pay him at Bhubaneswar. He had left Delhi on his summer vacation. I checked the ticket that Kakei handed me. It was a printed copy of an electronic transaction. I admired the automation in ticketing. I had been through situations where my confirmed paper ticket would be useless against the ferocity of the mob at the check in counter. Mobs and flashy shirts with sunglasses ruled the windows; no confirmation was guaranteed. Money would change hands discreetly. I felt extra grateful to Pradeep for having helped me and having done an important task for me to arrange a ticket. Kakei advised me to reserve a taxi for the flight time next day and I called the number he gave. I gave the apartment address and fixed three hours of lead-time.

I called various friends in Orissa to confirm the dates for the meetings and events. Friends are always special and childhood friends are extra special. In the new societies, people migrate out losing their connection to their birthplace and hometown. It is not clear if the separation is mutual. I do meet my friends, but not all that I would like to meet. One makes efforts to meet people. Meeting old friends brings happiness on both sides; it is the duty of the migrant to look for people. I have tried various types of reunions and they have been wonderful. One searches for the friends, finds them and reaches out. The task is not easy, there is change in people's lives; not everyone may be in a mood to join a reunion. Still many try to share a laugh together. Life is short; we live through the strength of our mutual friendship.

On this trip, I had tried to reach out to my friends in Delhi. Several of them had joined the Indian Administrative Service after qualifying through the competitive examinations. They go through the ladder and retire as high level civil servants. In Indian setup, the civil servants carry enormous influence though being always conditioned by the mood of some not-so-well-meaning politicians. Corruption enters the system easily and it is not clear where the origin is. The civil servants had to meet the demands of the politician such that the latter could stay in power. After subjugating themselves in various unsavoury ways, some civil servants themselves enter the fray of corruption.

My friends had survived the power game without being extra roughened. We were supposed to meet after I returned from Bhubaneswar. I had email communication with Gokul while leaving the US. Gokul was too happy to connect to me after forty-six years. My friend Prasanna had connected me to Gokul as a person who keeps track of other friends. I had met Prasanna a few times abroad. More importantly, I worked with him during his time as an official in routing the relief supplies after the super-cyclone in Orissa. I was visiting as a volunteer representing Oriyas abroad.

I called Gokul's number. While I called, his smartly dressed college appearance flashed before eyes. He came from Mayo College in Ajmer and joined us in our college elocution team. Several of us would gather at the local YMCA every Tuesday evening for a Toastmasters' Club meeting. A tall fatherly man Mr.R.K. Padhy and a dignified Oriya soldier Col. S. K. Roy would lead the Club meeting. I am unable to recall who engineered these meetings and how we got there. It used to be an extremely pleasant evening experience. Other students, senior to us would also join and we could be twenty strong in good days. We all benefited from the meetings. I recall the affectionate greetings of Mr. Padhy and Col. Roy all through my life. I have tried to teach and mentor youngsters in life, but to take other's children as one's own is a different art.

Gokul and I talked a bit about India and Orissa. He served the State Governments and at the Center in different capacities and took early retirement to pursue an independent career in consulting. He had built a good consulting business that took him to different countries on issues relating to food. I spoke to him about my impending visit to Chilika[8] Lake to determine the feasibility of monitoring the water conditions via a satellite. The Bay of Bengal remained mostly unexplored because of lack of international interest. Nationalistic strategy than science guides the geophysical research in the world. My visit would be exploratory. I had left Orissa thinking that I had a plan. Circumstance forces priorities. Newer challenges show up. They keep one occupied. I keep Orissa in my mind through my journey though it is not as lighted as when I was a student.

Time was passing by. I needed to do my prayer

---

[8]*The brackish water lake on the eastern seaboard of Orissa. It is the largest lake of its kind in Asia*

readings to seek blessings of the sixtieth wedding anniversary to my uncle and aunt. I took a shower and sat down at the shrine.

Home Shrine, Brigadier's family

I have wondered on the origin of prayer as a human tradition. One can speculate that wishful thinking is a human quality since there is freedom of action to make some wishes come true. A wish for good weather every day may be a perpetual human dream, but is granted only fifty percent of the time on an average. A wish elevates to a prayer when the weather remains bad for long periods of time; or when a man notices that a tree fell on a piece of property or on people. Man, prays to avert such falling tree episodes. When more knowledge comes in, man or woman possibly prays for good health in old age, upkeep of his/her children, and/or a peaceful demise. While we succeed in some of the wishes, most remain unfulfilled. It is possible we ask more than what we can handle. Reflective people discover that fulfilment of the wish is our acceptance of our environment. Lesser "we" become, more "fulfilled" we become!

Oriyas have developed their "triad plus one" cosmology. The triad consists of the body, the nature and time. They map to different labels in different cultures. The additional one is the will power, which can trump time. This last part is unique to the Jagannatha[9] form of the belief system where one is empowered with an option of escaping the falling tree by means of the force of will power. The will power is the conviction of internal sincerity, and is exhibited through the confidence gained in one's

---

[9] *A four-factor human cosmology based on body, nature, time and willpower.*

adventure in life. The will power is invoked through the singularity in purpose. There is a claim that prayers help, they help achieve this singularity. One has no objective success rate in the process except saying that the will favours the brave!

By observing her family wealth wither with the stroke of legislations in the newly independent country, and by being constrained to keep count of my father's engagement with the country's detention system because of his activism, my mother had possibly resorted to prayer as a defence. She would sing prayers to us and I would eventually learn. I had not seen my father praying, though I saw him doing my grandfather's last rites dutifully. His singing would mostly call for a perpetual will power and he could borrow lyric from any language with ease. People who left college during the struggle for India's freedom possibly ventured for an absolute win. My father celebrated the victory of man against all odds. He brought a new kind of prayer that declared redemption from ineptitude and inertia. He sang his heart out. The pitch of his voice could crack any barrier!

In India, prayers have many flavours. Sometimes they extol a creator to solicit a bit extra help; some other times they make admission of one's helplessness in the universe, a subset of which reminds one about humility as the noblest attribute. I like the latter type since I believe that all objects have a purpose to exist. Usurping humbler objects for individual gain is unethical in my opinion. Unfortunately, capitalism works the reverse way. I had not reconciled if the human frame was designed for the self or was made to be a part of a mutually respectful community. Since the last two thousand years, a good majority of the world had been taught to believe in an external boon-giver who waited to listen to a heart-felt prayer. There is competition in establishing the superiority of one's heart against another. Men appear in opulently designed costumes to claim superiority of their own hearts. In India, they do face and body painting to display their sincerity. Honesty in such operation has been an enigma to me. I do carry a piece of sanctified thread given to me by my grandfather. I have given such a thread to my son. We carry relics through our belief system!

In the early years in the US, I had attempted to socialize with people in different ethnic communities and had tried to expand on my interest in spoken languages and to enhance my reach in classical literature. While I was doing this to adjust my social skills, I was recruited to officiate in a cremation ritual. It was the first such Indian cremation ritual in Boston. The city did not have Hindu temples or Hindu priests. An old Hindu female person had died. Hindus believe that the body disintegrates to its elements than going places. I performed the ritual with my only skill in reading Sanskrit from a cleanly printed book. I suddenly gained reputation for my performance. I had to succumb to the pressure of officiating in new rituals as they appeared, and they appeared often. The pain of my ignorance in understanding mystery of life and death continued to increase. I have used prayer as an escape from admitting this ignorance.

I carried my prayer books to India while I travelled to perform my father's last rites. They have become a feature now in my home trips. I had come to believe that prayer helped to release tension. Sanskrit is constructed in a manner that the syllables can resonate to breath and I have enjoyed my efforts in recitation. Here I was sitting in front of the shrine in my uncle's home to offer my prayers. Possibly, I wished to demonstrate to my uncle and aunt that I cared. I produced my full-bodied recitation of the Gita and the Vedas. I did my reading for an hour with a lamp lighted in the corner.

After I finished, my uncle did his daily worship. He continues the tradition as held in our ancestral village at Puri. After he finished, we sat down for lunch. It was the crunch time in electric supply. The building power went down. The home had a battery-operated generator that switched on by default with limited capacity. We had to ration the power consumption of the fans in order to let the air conditioners operate. We retired to our respective rooms and tried to weather out the technological challenge.

A part of my goal in the trip was to check the strength of my body in adapting to the air of my childhood. Through age, I had discovered that air made human beings vulnerable to sickness. We feel good at mountaintops and enjoy the crispness of morning breeze. Urban air was dusty, it got heavy with fumes. I had noticed a remarkable change in air quality while I moved from the college town of Cambridge to the woods of Lincoln in Massachusetts. Urban centres are created to operate through enclosed halls where air can be controlled. I loved my outdoor walks. I wished to check urban outdoors in India.

With the power supply, indoors being tight, I thought of sneaking out to check the streets. I decided against keeping the door unlocked and planned on returning after an hour when my uncle might have finished resting. Getting down to the street was like entering Drona's battle formation. Going forward is easy but one may not be able to return. One can easily get lost in the "left"s and "right"s. Taxi stands would have temporal change following the shade and all buildings might look alike. I decided on making limited turns, and observed my path carefully. As

I walked forward, I got a buoyancy sensation of lifting hot air. The bright sun simmered. There was less traffic; the air was heavy. I saw on left a man taking a haircut in the open sky with a mirror tucked on a fence wall. I marvelled at the ingenuity of using sidewalk for business in the hot sun!

I saw a locked up Jaina[10] temple with an elaborate list of "don'ts" prominently displayed. The Temple covered good amount of space and looked rich. I have been puzzled by the theory in the Jaina faith. It is not practiced with the rigor that it was originally intended. Most Jains are business people who act as intermediaries in markets while always keeping an eye not to directly kill insects or animals. They compensate profit making by building schools and hospitals. It is a great compromising faith. The principles fit well to Indian style of individual capitalism. Jainism brought acceptance as a trait in Indian culture. The faith teaches mutual respect. I have admired the tenets of Jainism.

I was at the next street intersection. I contemplated sitting down, but there was no bench or a café. Some squatted on the ground, some others sat on platform planks of shut down stores. A woman arrived to my left with a bag in her hand. She squatted on the ground a few feet from me. She put a few bricks in a geometric shape and put a metal wire mesh on top. She got charcoal from her bag and placed them on the wire mesh. Then she tried to light a fire by burning some newspapers underneath the wire mesh. The whole construction could be one square foot. A van came by and parked on the side. A man came

---

[10] *An old India faith possibly predating the Vedas. The faith preaches von-violence as the fundamental principle.*

out with another bag and a young lad jumped towards the woman. The boy hugged the woman and asked if he could help run the fire. The woman agreed, the boy started blowing air under the charcoal. The boy's tiny, flexible frame was perfect for the task. While I readied myself to witness some magic tricks, the man squatted down. He removed a few corn cobs out of his bag. He got busy in removing the husks. I was amazed with the cooperative family operation. I was not sure if the van was purchased through the family enterprise. Golden cobs with black pimples were garnished with lemon and butter. I felt like waiting to get a baked corn cob, but the dust on the road was an inhibitor.

    I had to end my expedition; it was getting late. I retraced my path and was delighted that I had not veered. The turn at the main road was important since the side lanes were always hidden away. I reached back to the fifth-floor apartment and pressed the bell. My uncle opened the door and I went in to the relative coolness of the darkened living quarters. I told him of my street adventure; he warned me with the published news of the heat strokes. I did feel dryness in my eyes and tried to splash water on them. I drank some lemon water to cool down.

    Seema is Kakei's second daughter whom I had not met in Delhi yet. She has long days with commute and work. Transportation in Delhi is not easy. My uncle wanted me to visit Seema's mother-in-law, the Brigadier's widow. The Brigadier was a well-decorated soldier and had an apartment in the special Army enclave for retired soldiers. He had died a few years back. Seema's husband was in real estate business. He collapsed suddenly last February with a massive stroke. He came home in the evening and wanted a special supper. He asked the housekeeper to cook his favourite recipe to order. Then in a few minutes, he dropped with a thud at the doorsteps. Life is too fragile; he did not turn sixty. His mother Mrs. Chopra, the widow, had suffered a stroke the previous year. The housekeeper assisted her. The husband, Seema and their two children lived in Brigadier's house with the widow. Seema's older daughter graduated from the School of Fashion Design in Ahmedabad and worked as a freelance designer. She worked with readymade clothes and her selections were featured in trade magazines. The boy finished Law School, and was admitted to the Bar in Delhi.

Seema volunteered to come to pick me up. Kakei had suggested I talk to the children. I had offered that we go out for supper where we might talk in a relaxed environment. Seema had a driver. While I was in the US, Seema was helping me with the planning of the sixtieth wedding anniversary fete that was cancelled. She showed up and we travelled. She seemed popular with her friends. She was getting a number of phone calls. She had taken her husband's death in stride but was protective of her children. She was a military daughter-in-law and everything for her was matter of fact!

I saw Brigadier Chopra's name etched in big capitals in a bronze plaque. The Army decoration of Param Vishisht Seva Medal[11] was mentioned underneath. We entered the house. Adi had a light beard and had features like the two nephews I left behind in London. His sister Mahi joined in. We chatted a bit; I saw Mahi's work in various magazines. I complimented her design work. Then I went

---

[11] *A high-level decoration awarded to defense personnel in India.*

to meet Mrs. Chopra. It was an honour to meet a Brigadier's wife. She was tall, handsome, dignified. It is said a man is known through his wife. Mrs. Chopra lived it. Being paralyzed in leg through a stroke, she needed a walker to move. I proceeded to touch her feet and sat next to her. She belonged to the Arya Samaj[12] and strongly believed in the Arya Samaj principles. We talked about family, life, India and the US. I admired her demeanour. Any remorse was hidden miles deep. A military person lived in the present. SriKrishna was a military man.

Departure from Delhi

It was June 23, Saturday. I had to take a flight in the afternoon to Bhubaneswar. Morning tea was done and we talked about the extended family. As we grew older, even the family members get detached. The Gita said that detachment is the best way to live life. Detachment is not meant to withdraw from people, but remain detached while being with one's people. Some monks and holy men run away from home and make their living with other apparently like-minded persons. Running away reduces responsibility and makes the person free from obligations to family and friends. Some join groups and then compete with other similar groups. Some aspire to become the chief in their group. Aspiration rarely dies in detachment. Experimenting detachment while in the group is a test of human conduct. Kakei seemed to have figured it out.

In a family setting, we take beatings of betrayal, abuse and anger. To keep peace in a larger family is a difficult task. In early times, agriculture and food kept people

---

[12] *A Hindu group who do not believe in the teachings of the Vedas and avoid physical forms of the deities.*

together. These days one person can feel superior to another by carrying some trivial tokens or high-sounding labels. In Orissa, many large families were fraught with disharmony because of mutual rivalry among family members. Strong traditional families had been devastated under the pressure of jealousy and greed. Restlessness due to insecurity crippled the once prosperous society. Mutual hatred had become a passion. One's own brother or sister became easy targets. There was no social counselling; there was little spiritual education. People easily contrived crooked and selfish plots. Kakei was SriKrishna in the Gita talking to a nephew to educate.

We skipped our morning walk and I went to my room to do my packing. I located two gift items I had carried for Kakei and Khudi: a pen for him and a collapsible travel bag for her. They accepted my gifts with affection. We spoke a bit about economy and life. It was not easy to live as an old person in India unless one had a pension. There was no social security, and one operated from the savings. Kakei had used up his savings in buying the apartment. His son helped him with occasional subsistence. The apartment was a good investment and had appreciated in time. Kakei boasted that with five floors, theirs was the tallest building in the area. It was the only one graced with an elevator. I figured that the real estate in Delhi could be more expensive than in New York.

I called Rabi Dash, a down-to-earth associate of my father who was undertaking the efforts of collecting, compiling and publishing my father's writings. He came from a coterie of admirers who loved my father's style of living and his literature. All progressive young people in the 40's, 50's and '60s possibly sang his songs, but to archive materials was not a simple task. Most of the material stayed in people's mouths, and was reproduced from memory in recitation. I sang the songs, but rarely understood the thrust. Now I admired them. Not many know the diction in Oriya, and not many have a feel for the Orissa soil. People need to study my father to gain entry into the use of Oriya language. The language was old; the constructs were unique; the metaphors were special. A lot research is required to track the origin of Oriya diction.

Rabi Dash had maintained his life as a pragmatist and an activist. He lived in his village Tarpur, fifty miles away from Bhubaneswar and commuted by bus every day. At Bhubaneswar, he operated a store that sold material woven by hand by the indigenous people in rural Kalahandi. Kalahandi was a drought-prone area. He undertook the task of digging ponds to capture rainwater. He was the tribal peoples' liaison to the Government and presented their grievances to the media. I had known him from my college days through a Gandhi Study Forum that he ran. I admired his work. I supported him in whatever way I could. I sponsored the book publishing, but it was a labour love by him.

Kakei had been patiently observing me with my schedule preparation. He finally prodded me to take a shower. It was about 12:30 PM. I took a shower and had a quick lunch. The taxi arrived at 1:30 PM and it was time to leave. I hugged Khudi and Kakei. I dragged my luggage to the elevator. Kakei followed me. He was always practical. My admiration to him had increased during the past few days. I could feel from his eyes that he would miss me. I told him that I would be back in two weeks. I hugged him again.

Delhi Airport

Alaknanda to Delhi airport was about an hour's ride.

I was now somewhat familiar with the road signs and the road. I had been to Delhi many times but never seen a map of the city. All I knew was that the city was spread out over fifty or more miles. New satellite towns were springing up to handle business and product manufacture. As we moved, I saw in an intersection a street name General Abdal Nasser Marg. I had seen earlier Josip Broz Tito Marg. These were Nehru's handicraft. He had taken these leaders as allies and developed the group of non-aligned nations. The goal was not to tilt either to the US or to the Soviet Union. India was the leader of these nations by being the largest, and the most vocal. The voice was tampered when China attacked India in 1962. It went further down in the conflict with Pakistan in 1966. India tilted to the Soviet Union, the tilt getting more through the Bangladesh war in 1971. India now remained friendly both to the US and Russia, but was apprehensive about the moves from China. Pakistan's government was always unstable; it was not clear to understand the moves there. Some Pakistanis appeared to behave as born rivals to Indians.

  I saw big signs in blue of different areas in Delhi and settled myself that we were in the right direction. The familiar highway showed up and we headed towards the Terminal 1 that catered to the domestic flights. The taxi dropped me off at the curb and the driver put my luggage in a cart. The floor was newly done, the cart moved smoothly. I arrived at the glass door to show my papers for entry. The man checking the gate had a large gun tucked at his back. He looked like a hybrid between a police and a soldier. He took his own time to examine my e-ticket and my passport. Possibly, he was briefed to be extra careful with the foreigners. India had suffered through its liberal entry hospitality. I appreciated the caution. I thought bare eyes are not the right tools for the job. He did not use any magnifying glass.

Young women were handling the Indigo counter. They were dressed in western style uniforms; India had become international. They were courteous and friendly. Many other young women walked around with walkie-talkies stuck to their lips and they were in constant communication to some other inner controls. India has work force. It could do things by human intelligence what is done by cameras and sensors abroad. My turn came at the counter. The luggage was weighed. I had forgotten that the luggage could give hiccup if the international flight was not continued through the domestic routes. This has happened before. This time there was no problem. I only carried small gifts for my friends. My parents have passed away; my mother is not there to welcome me home. It would be an accomplishment if I can protect my parents' memory.

The flight was scheduled for 4:30 PM. I had some time left. I took a chair in an area waiting for the security to call my flight. I looked around to observe people. The nature and stature of people did not look any different from a railway platform; the similar pattern of multiple bags, not so robust packing, people sitting next to piles of luggage. The children were being fed; the elders spoke in many strange sounding languages. India was an open society; conversations could be loud. No one was reading a book, or a newspaper; there were no bookstalls. I did not want to appear different. Some people showed up in wheel chairs, their relatives attended to them. I closed my eyes a bit; it was early morning for me back in the US.

The Security called and I checked through. The guards were polite. There is a natural friendliness in Indian guards. In the US, they have a new guard group who seem to be mad all the time. They do not act like average American who is friendly. It is said that there is genuine anger among some people to hurt the US. It would seem as hurting the US could be their life's goal. The guards protect the aircraft. Nobody wants to be blown up high in the air; we succumb to the searches. In India, I found it subjective, they did not hassle everyone. They had just changed rule for people over 75 in the US; it makes the law civil. In India touching or stripping is not done. These cultural values could change in future.

Another security check was done at the gate and we were loaded to a bus for a hundred-yard journey to the aircraft. Like other things in India, the cabin did not look the most robust. The seats were tight and the cushions were hard. India's adoption of technology was for convenience. The transports had good engines. The taxis I rode in Delhi had seen middle age, but still ran optimally. The body is inconsequential, what you need is a good heart!

Flight to Bhubaneswar

I had a window seat. The next person was a young man flying home from London. He had been requested to come home not to miss the big auspicious wedding season. Apparently, no such schedule would show up for six months. For a successful wedding and a prosperous life, astrological predictions had become important. Some people made money through these fortune-telling operations. The greatest sponsor in Zee TV cabled from India to the US is an astrologer. His slogan is that "astrology and numerology combined makes a great prediction." Many fall in trap. It is strange that so many are vulnerable. People think astrology would help fix stress in life.

Astrological predictions came from the Greeks and the Arabs who speculated on the time of day to launch an attack. In India, everything might look like an attack. Stepping out is as if launching an attack! You must check your auspicious time before launching any action. My young friend spoke of his life in London, his living, work and the cricket games. He was happy with his income, but was lonely in London. He felt homesick.

It was time for the airline hospitality. Food as a service rates an airline. I was not hungry; just wanted some tea. The tea was lousy, nothing like what I had in the morning. I read my newspaper and learned more about the corruption, the scandals and the protests. The stalwarts of protests were a seventy- four-year-old farmer who spoke of Gandhi and had acquired some ambitious followers, and a red colour dressed militant yogi who was empowered by huge money his followers had raised for him. It was a strange couple. The culprits could be anyone walking on the street. They were talking about astronomical numbers in black money. Money was funnelled out to be out of country safe havens. This was an old game, possibly enhanced when the late Rajiv Gandhi came to power. When you are not prepared to work for the people, you look for your own security. People in power try to cover it up. The Prime minister said he was not involved, which was probably true. Then we search to find out who did it, not easy!

ORISSA

Arrival, meeting the sick brother

We reached Bhubaneswar. The single strip airport has always pained me as the symbol of my people's poverty. That one could fly when seventy percent starved was a convenience hidden in that single strip. It was not clear if other States got more revenue than Orissa. I did not understand why the infrastructure was so poor, if it was mismanagement or if there was lack of management. Have we turned to be the most corrupt State? I had heard that Bihar was worse. I had travelled to Ranchi and taken flights from there. They seemed to have style and substance. In Bhubaneswar, we did not use a bus to come to the flight; we just walked up and down, plain and simple. We were lucky that the flight arrived every day. Earlier it was twice a week. I was told that most officers were corrupt, the ministers did not care. The Chief Minister even did not speak the local Oriya language!

I picked up my luggage and slowly walked out. My sister Lakhi and her husband were supposed to pick me up. I did not see them and waited. There was no obvious place to wait. Everyone spoke loud on the cell phone. The noise decibel was high. I observed and lingered; nobody asked me a question. In earlier trips, somebody would ask if I needed help. Now everybody was busy in reaching his or her destination. Cars and taxis passed by. Shouts were made on the phone to the subservient for their apparent irresponsibility in not showing up. Flattery was conveyed on the telephone announcing arrival and scheduling prospective meetings. It was a good street play. We used to go to Calcutta to watch acted street plays; here it was real time. There was no theme, just noise.

I had a brother next to me; his name was Ajoy. He passed away before reaching ten years of age. My parents were shocked. To lose a child is utmost pain; my father did everything to save his life. The prominent physician BC Roy from Calcutta would visit him. He had a bad lever; the body would swell up and turn yellow. I remember the wailing of my mother the day he breathed his last. She would ask me to get firewood thinking that heat would wake him up. It was late in the afternoon when my uncles took the body for burial. Young bodies are not cremated in Hindu belief. I wanted to accompany the body to the cemetery, but my uncles would not take me.

The next one among my siblings is Apu, the physician at Rourkela. Her son lived in London. The other nephew was the son of my brother Sanjoy, whom I was visiting. Sanjoy had developed a pituitary tumour, which we had surgically removed in Boston. Apparently, the tumour had developed early in his life, nobody knew about it. He came for higher studies to the US. The pain became severe in a month and we discovered the tumour. A kind physician friend connected me to a neurosurgeon and it was a miracle that we could schedule a surgery. This was 1990. He would be on steroids for the rest of his life but he would be productive.

After my mother passed away and his son left for London, Sanjoy had felt terribly lonely. He had developed some heart problem. On a November night in 2009 he got dizzy on the steps to the upper floor; he rolled down several steps, and hit ground hard. His wife worked night shift in the newspaper and there was little help. He was escorted to his room by some bystanders who could not diagnose the trauma. His wife came in the morning and tried the emergency procedures. Through sheer luck and determination, Sanjoy survived. His cognitive faculties were returning. He was a courageous man, the best among us. I wanted to see him; I wanted to hug him.

After many turns, we reached his place. It was a rented apartment, convenient for the hospitals in Bhubaneswar. I entered. I went near his bed and tried to speak to him. He opened his eyes, looked at me. His eyes got moist. He was not able to get up by himself; nor could he speak. There was a nurse's aide standing next to him. She stayed full time attending to him. His body looked robust; he had a big head. Sanjoy, the big boy, who led processions at the age of nine riding on the shoulders of elders, was lying helpless on a bed. He was a dynamic, eloquent man. He had piercing eyes. He had my father's voice, now quietened! Human expression is an inner call. Call to action is a different breed. I sang prayers to him, stroked his head. I pressed his arms and took his palm to mine. He pressed them back and I loved the handshake. He was the one who took care of me any time I was home. This would be the first time I would miss his company in my trip. He was my guide and escort. I thought deep, my world was possibly narrowing. It is called nature's play, always mysterious.

DAY - 1

BHUBANESWAR

Family recollection

We left Sanjoy's house and merged on the highway. It was the usual traffic of Bhubaneswar, less chaotic than Delhi. For the first time, I was proceeding to stay overnight away from my parental home after having landed in Orissa. I was supposed to help run the family, but it was not easy for me to deal with the absence of my parents. I needed protection.

My father was a romantic man. Such men possess huge talents and high creativity; they are lofty in their ideals. They stay passionate to life and they love the world around them. They assume people's problems. It took me a long time to understand the phrase *para peera*[13] "pain of others" in the Narsinh Mehta[14] song. Yoga is not to feel sympathy; it is to experience the pain. It is an inner quality. My father's

---

[13] *A phrase popularized through Mahatma Gandhi's appreciation of a devotional song written by Narsi Mehta.*

[14] *A fifteenth century singer-poet from Gujarat known for his heart-touching lyrics.*

parents adored him; he was extra special because of his manners, conduct and personality. The ideas of equality of men in society appealed to him as a young man. He had joined the young Communist group in Orissa. Jail terms followed in quick succession; the family thought to get him married to make him a householder. This was 1945. My mother came from a Diwan's[15] house. The newfound liberty on the street was like Valmiki's Sita going picnic in the forest. In 1946, college students led by my father mauled the Union Jack. Things got rough. My parents were determined to wade through. I was born in 1947, a few days before India's independence. My mother kept accounts of every penny those days including the days she was in the hospital!

We used to live in a rental apartment in Chhatrabazar[16] at Cuttack and it was the hub of the local progressive activity. I recall the nights I would go with my mother to meet my father who would be hiding in the distant paddy fields outside the local villages. He was the people's man. People would drop off food and stuff in our house. He used to get a small remuneration as a Communist party worker, and had some revenue from his writings. He argued his habeas corpus and succeeded in releasing himself from detention along with his associates. Then he ran for Parliament from Puri constituency in 1952. He was the favourite to win the seat but the counting of votes was bungled; ballot boxes were stolen away. It was the pang of the new democracy. There was no Carter to watch the balloting. My father

---

[15] A counsellor to the King, an administrative position engineered by the British during the colonial period.
[16] A neighbourhood in Cuttack known for warehouses and vegetable markets.

had become a respected orator. His words had a message for the State. He could mesmerize an audience of thousands by the eloquence of his oratory. He would sing powerful liberation songs composed by him. He was an artist. His lyrics continue to remain etched in people who heard him in those early years after India's independence.

Sponsored by the World Peace Council he went on a tour of the Communist and left-leaning countries in 1955 and made a name for himself by reciting Oriya on Soviet radio. He returned to participate in the massive State Reformation movement in 1956. Those were the tumultuous days in Orissa. People were in high adrenaline. The agitators won, Orissa's boundary was redrawn. Oriya language was adopted for the administrative purposes. In the Fall of that year, the Soviet tanks crossed the borders of Hungary and crushed the people's revolt there. My father had sleepless nights. He was confused, disillusioned. His romanticism did not have space for tanks against the masses. The pressure of the household was also possibly taking a toll. My mother was pregnant with the fifth child. Going was tough at home; they were seeing the realities of the forest! My father was invited to take the job as the Orissa correspondent for the newspaper Anandabazar Patrika[17] of Calcutta. He accepted and tried to gain an income. This helped us to move to a larger space in Ranihat. I picked up a bit of Bengali language.

I was with my father when he met Pandit Nehru in Nagpur in 1959. He came back to organize the socialist block inside the Congress party. Resources were given to him. A new newspaper called Kalinga was initiated. He

---

[17] *A Bengali newspaper from Kolkata, India, in operation for about a hundred years.*

was appointed the Editor. Biju Patnaik became the Chief Minister of Orissa. There was corruption in the government; my father wanted his freedom to run the newspaper. The club mentality in the State administration bothered him; he was critical. Misappropriation of State funds was rampant; he had to write about it. Vanity and power were not for him. The older political leaders were dying or aging, he was getting lonely.

His new-found success evaporated one night through a short letter. The newspaper management had "realized" that he was not suitable for their whitewash; he was removed from the newspaper. Nehru died in 1964 when on a visit to Orissa. It was sudden. Those were sad days. My father was depressed. He took some time to recover and went back to the fields of toil that he enjoyed. He would organize labour; he would explain to them their rights. They would treat him as a messiah; they would give him subsistence. He would go for lengthy periods of hunger strikes in support of the labour.

The old Orissa stalwart Nabakrushna Chowdhury visited him. They tried to create a new Left Front. My father kept soft corner for the Marxists in the Communist movement. The Soviet block was unreliable and possibly disintegrating. He contested elections from the Bhubaneswar Parliamentary Constituency in 1967. I served as the election manager. Out of seven Assembly constituencies, we won four, but lost large in the other three. Some areas were inaccessible and I do not know how they did polling there. Elections need large amount of money and strong resources. Money used could be an investment; for the victor, the returns are possibly multi-fold. People who contributed knew how to collect!

My father wanted to experiment the life of an ordinary

man. But the ordinary man did not go very far in India. It was a disorderly capitalist society. One needed money to survive. He produced books, poetry and texts; his in-laws and family helped. To maintain the household of nine was a hard task. I had scholarships that we would use for home. Everything was drying up; idealism in the country was dying. I do not know if any one interviewed him to check his personal views those days. He was a loving affectionate father who felt for the little children whose fathers broke sweat in the mines to create money for the wealthy. He would spend long hours with the new youth motivating them to serve people. He would dream that things would turn soon; my mother would be scrounging grocery to fix supper.

He had helped his brothers to be educated and they were successfully employed. I joined employment in 1968 and helped what I could. I came to know the plight of many writers and scholars in Orissa. I got the conviction that creativity demanded actual physical experience. One had to scar one's heart to write about the scars in people. The thrust of language did not come if one was not free. How does a man become free? The society wants man to be bonded, to be sold. I met EMS Namboodiripad[18] of Kerala in one of the election meetings in Rourkela. I loved the man; I loved his language. He had less encumbrances, no family to tow. EMS was a worker and a leader, but he was not observing the world as a poet. A poet needs a home, a family to share food, a wife to dream. The passions are different for a poet than those for a leader. My father was a poet-leader. He wanted to live the life of the objects that he could write about.

I had returned from the US to work in India, but

---

[18] *The first Communist politician elected as the State Chief Minister in India. Also known as EMS.*

had no luck. I left back in 1974 with the determination of saving the family and experiment with life in my way. My father understood; he cooperated. One deal I made with him, no more jail terms! Let the sly have their pie; let the corrupt drink their wine. We would stand up as a family than dropping out; we would be free. My brother Sanjoy stood up with me and he worked. Then came the younger brother Abhi and we were a relay team. My sister Apu became a physician and she remained the supervisor in health. The three younger ones needed nurturing and they continued in school. My mother continued to be the tower of dignity and strength.

The need at Cuttack was higher than what I could remit; paying rent was hard. Father decided to move to a piece of property that he had procured in Chauliaganj where we had built a few rooms. This was 1981. Life moved and we tried to save money to help complete the house. Abhi was in the US and left for Cuttack in 1998 to help complete the structure. The free man could live in a house he owned! When I showed up in 1999, my father was ecstatic that he was living in his own house. He showed me around how well everything was done. He wanted everything to be done with one's own sweat; and he felt happy that it was. He had done much new writings by that time, but nobody was keeping track. I did not have the depth in Oriya. Rabi Dash made efforts to bring out a poetry collection in 2000. My father proudly titled it Quomi-Nara[19]. He called me to express his pleasure when the book was released in March, 2000.

In the struggle for putting things together and facing

---

[19] " *Voice of the people*" – slogan developed by the Indian National Army during the Freedom Movement.

challenges in operating with dignity and freedom in a different world, I was a lonely traveller. I was unable to keep track of my father's genius. He wrote for magazines, for brochures and on scraps of paper. He knew his diction; that was his heart. Rabi Dash brought out a book collecting one hundred of his most popular poems in 2007. Last Spring I received the electronic copy of the book on the practice and science of Oriya language. This was first published in 1971. I was stunned to read the depth of analysis in the book. Having seen many scholars in the world and having worked with some, my father appeared to me in a completely different class. The analysis was splendid. It was new and novel. That he had the vision of educating the masses on the intricacies of space sciences. That he was trying to find a language for the task was thrilling to me. This was a different man than I knew as my father. I wanted to read everything he might have written. I had gained some qualification having read and translated Sarala Dasa meanwhile; I had gained some tools to calibrate writing and scholarship. The plan was there to release a new edition of my father's book on linguistics book during my trip.

    We reached my sister's house. They had designated their guest bed in the living room for me. I spread my wares and took some food. I spoke with the girls and learned about the wedding preparation. Everything was going on plan. The groom was from Lucknow and the party would arrive in a few days. The wedding would take place in the night of June 29th. I was given a well-designed wedding invitation card. Weddings in India are special and the activity is chaotic. I was happy that my sister was not counting pennies as my mother had to. Where was the poet? Can he feed the village leaving some food for himself?

DAY - 2

CHILIKA

Travel to Chilika, Laboratory, *Bhagabati*[20] Temple

It was Sunday, June 24. Bhubaneswar was cooler than Delhi. The monsoons had dropped rains. I heard that the temperature had been as hot as in Delhi and had lately cooled. Rains are good for the farmlands, but Bhubaneswar has poor drainage. A little rain creates traffic problem. Water does not drain away. It stays on to trickle down. The problem worsens as ground gets saturated. Water on the road can stay for hours; floods occur.

The morning tea ritual at Bhubaneswar was not so significant. My sister wanted to be a good host. I saw her as the little kid whom I carried as a baby. Memory images are strange; they stay frozen. I had to leave early for Chilika. My young friend Nagen would accompany me. We were scheduled to leave at 7:30 in the morning. Nagen showed up. He asked if he could leave his motorbike at my sister's house. Our plan was to go to Sanjoy's house and there we

---

[20] *A local manifestation of Devî, worshipped as a deity by Oriyas.*

were supposed to pick up the car. Sanjoy's wife Gita has invested in a car, but does not drive herself. She hires a driver as and when needed. The driver Mali worked for the same newspaper where Gita worked. He moonlighted as a driver in need. Apparently, the "rent a driver" practice was common; taxi transportation was expensive.

We took an auto-rickshaw. I found the rickshaw must have the divine engine to operate on any terrain. It negotiated ditches and slopes, it took water and mud. It manoeuvred curves in precision, it never stopped; I thought it was an amazing piece of hardware. It was not clear why there were ditches and muddy water everywhere. Some ditches were permanent. Just before reaching my brother's house there was the Khyber Pass; you would need solid tires to hold grip. A novice rider like me could be ejected from the rickshaw! The intelligent in me learned to hold the rails tight such that the passenger was not thrown out. There were no attempts to repair the road; somebody has usurped the money. People in the Government did not look at these "small" matters. People who usurped money brought votes.

Nagen and I reached my brother's house. Sundays were a bit easier on Gita. She worked six days a week, now had taken the day shift. She kept a watch on Sanjoy, who was susceptible to minor changes in air and dust. He was having long stays in the hospital because of infection. Then they discovered that the hospital caused the infection. Gita had installed air filters and wire screens. She monitored air quality in the room. They had learned that a cough or a sneeze was an indication of air pollution. Everybody must wash hands before entering the room. People in direct contact with the patient must use rubber gloves. They were diligent caregivers. I admired the protocol.

Mali finally called about 9:30 AM and said that he could show up by 11 AM. He had been away on a different job and had not forgotten our assignment. Gita coaxed him to rush, but it was a seller's market. He said he would take public transportation. He claimed it would be no different from the rickshaw transportation. Given the road conditions, I thought his estimate was not off the mark. We waited. He did show up at 11 and we were ready to leave. Our plan was to stay overnight at Chilika and return back the next day evening after traveling through the hinterland. Mali was ready with his bag.

Road to Chilika

The road to Chilika was the National Highway #5 (lately renumbered as #16) that connected Kolkata to Chennai. It was a two-lane highway. We went via the caves of Khandagiri and Udayagiri and reached Khurdha. I had travelled these roads at length during the election work in 1967. These are areas of highly fertile lands washed by numerous rivers, big and small. Here the human settlement was prehistoric. The farmers had risen against the British much before anyone else did. They had fought against Ashoka[21] two thousand years before the revolt against the British. The fight against the British had the same characteristic as of farmers in Concord lining up against the Red Coats. Crushing the Khurdha rebellion took some effort on the part of the British and they kept away from Orissa as much as possible. The British were the rulers. The neglect and exploitation of Orissa had begun.

The scenery became beautiful green. There were paddy fields on both sides. There were villages far away

---

[21] *An emperor in north who invaded Orissa around 300BC.*

beyond the tree line. Not much traffic on the road, not much activity in the field; new plants were coming up. My jet lag had not fully receded. I felt dizzy by noontime. Nagen and I talked haltingly about the road. I had been dozing off. After an hour, we came through a pass between two hills, famously called Mamu (uncle) and Bhanaja (nephew) in Orissa. I did not know the legend behind the names; they were the gatekeepers to Chilika. We could see water to our left, the tranquil feeling of expanse of bluish green waters as far as eye could see. It was special, a big pond with sun sparkling on little wavelets.

Chilika is a brackish water lake. Several rivers from the Mahanadi delta drain to Chilika in the north. Many small seasonal rivers drain in the south. The lake opens to the sea with a narrow mouth of half mile width while it spreads forty miles long and twelve miles wide. Water enters the lake at high tide bringing new sea water to mix with the river water. An interesting water mass develops for the aquatic species. The bird resting over the lake in the spring is a sight to behold. Thousands of birds would be lying on the still waters of the lake and their fluttering with the rise of morning sun is a cosmic sight. I had accompanied my parents as a child to visit Chilika. Childhood memories capture our imagination.

This time I was in Chilika as a satellite scientist. I had developed interest in the world water masses and their characterization for scientific understanding. The water-colour is a function of water mixing and upwelling, and can be used as a good indicator of the gross changes in the atmosphere above. Earth's weather and climate remain a problem for man to tackle. Oceans are a major controlling factor. I had worked on instrumentation that can discriminate small changes on the surface while observing hundreds of miles up. My goal was to check if we could convince the sponsors to use such instruments over Chilika with suitable flight trajectories carrying the spectral instrument on an aircraft.

We were on the road. We were not sure how to reach the guesthouse that would host us for the night. There was a road bifurcation and we assumed the road to the left would be right. We took that. Nothing much happened for many miles; then we saw a sign for the Marine Research Laboratory. It said that the guesthouse was further down. After going through a small bazaar area, we reached a freshly painted two- storey-building complex with adjacent single storey buildings. We saw the lake behind the building. It felt nice. The manager had rooms for us and gave us three sets of keys. We went to our respective rooms, had a wash and quickly gathered to take lunch in the cafeteria.

Marine Laboratory

The lunch was cooked to order. Orissa rice was different from Delhi rice, looked more gathered up than crystalline. The lentil preparation dal was great, just right for my Oriya taste. There was a mixed vegetable and some fried vegetable. A television news program was running reporting about the extremist problems in western Orissa. The insurgent Naxalites had kidnapped some members of the legislature keeping everyone on guard. The Kandha[22] in Orissa were a fighting breed; some young activists had made them politically aware of their sorry economic state. The tribal people love their land. Everyone must respect it; abusers must be killed. Extremism in Orissa has reason to be homebred.

---

[22] *An old indigenous tribe that has habitat in the western hills of Orissa.*

We were supposed to meet the scientific staff at the Laboratory at 2:30 PM and we rushed. Several young people greeted us and informed us that the Chief Scientist was on his way from Bhubaneswar. We visited the displays in the lab and saw many special aquatic species preserved in glass jars. I read the legends and felt happy that scientific work was being pursued. A young researcher led us to their computer lab where he displayed modelling results for us. A flow code from a Dutch lab had been made available to them and they were applying it to simulate the Chilika conditions in tracking the saltwater inlet from the sea and its movement in the lagoon. It was a good first order model and gave insight on the salinity and pH at various points in the basin. They would make the application more realistic gradually.

The Chief Scientist arrived. We had discussions about the work in the Laboratory. He showed me various bathymetry charts and reports of the buoy measurements they monitored. He was interested in the habitat of various species and looked for marine population changes as a function of the water condition and silting. He had charts of fresh water inflow from dozens of rivers draining to the lake from north and the west. He had plans to make systematic studies of salinity and correlate it to fish migration and to fish habitat. He mentioned about the research vessel of the Laboratory and offered invitation to take a ride inside the lake. I accepted the invitation, but it was too late to go in water. The fishing boats folded their nets in the late afternoon. One had to avoid entanglement. We would go in the morning. I felt curious about the marine process. I looked for brochures and publications from the lab. He told me that there was a big Conference the next day and I could pick up materials at that time. He invited me to attend the Conference.

Visit to Banapur

It was going to be 4 PM. I had planned to visit the nearby *Bhagabati* Temple that my mother admired. It was in Banapur, which was on a side road ten miles earlier. We turned car as to return and found the road to the town. The area looked prosperous. Banapur is a cultural place; it was the capital of a prosperous dynasty of the Shailodhavas[23] in the early years. There was active maritime trade with far away islands of modern day Indonesia. Oriyas had established a kingdom there. Those were the days of strong Shakti worship in Orissa. The animal sacrifice is a ritual in many such temples in Orissa. *Bhagabati* temple is a major Shakti symbol. A massive protest by the animal right advocates bringing an injunction order from the High Court helped stop the ritual of animal sacrifice. It was said that the Mother *Bhagabati* granted boons when animals were sacrificed. Some of the western scholars get fascinated with such rituals and create commentaries around them. Sacrifice is an old human psychological condition. Somewhere else they sacrificed human beings!

After winding our way through we reached the Temple. We parked on the side lane; a man somewhat tipsy said that he would keep an eye on the car. We had to settle, not much we could do. We washed our feet and entered the Temple. We first went around the Temple perimeter. There were small shrines set on the Temple wall with a priest standing at each shrine. The priests explained the mythology of the scenes depicted at the respective shrines. They parroted some mythology books and they expected money. At the third shrine,

---

[23] *A regime famed for their foreign trade and temple construction.*

the priest was intoxicated. The scene disturbed me. It was a scene of substance abuse. I admonished the man and did not listen to his story. Fortunately, he did not pursue us.

We bought a few clay lamps and offered lighted lamps at the main shrine. The shrine certainly needed a good clean up. I felt sad about the deterioration of faith and heritage. The place of worship is a gauge of the confidence of people. It appeared that consumer base had increased and there were not many sponsors. The priests seemed nominal and did not evoke respect and faith. An old tradition was withering.

We came back to the main road and took a tea break. There was a roadside stand. It was a family business, run by two brothers. Income was seasonal, margin of profit was small. They said there was little buying power in people. They cater mostly to the visitors who came in winter and spring for bird watching. The owner served tea in tiny glasses. It was of good quality. We paid. They did not expect any gratuity; we did not offer any. I watched people coming in; there was a small crowd. I thought to engage in a conversation, but my friends were eager to get back to the Guest House. We took to the road.

Chilika Guesthouse

Nagen is a resourceful person. He had arranged in the Cafeteria that the evening food be served in the room. I washed my face and sat down to follow Orissa news on television. The news items were old; news production is slow. I switched to a channel that gave folk and devotional music. I have interest in these. The artists were new. The melody was there in the production but the expression did not come out right. I had developed interest on phonetics and phonology. Words possibly had meanings inherent in the expression. I had heard that such theories were developed in eastern India, possibly some scholars inquired the source of human expression. The shakti[24] manifestation is our association with sound. Once we tune to the tone we may gain out-of-body experience. There is a metaphysical aspect that we hear the sound that we produce later. We become the channels through which the cosmos expresses itself.

After I had my meal, the house phone rang. The man at the desk said that there was a problem and my two friends must vacate their rooms. Some new guests had arrived and they would need accommodation! I called Nagen and Mali to squeeze in my room for the night. I was new, and we were guests. I did not know what to expect. They brought over their bags and we made a dormitory out of the large double bed. After we had reset ourselves, telephone again rang saying that the rooms were not required and my friends could go back. We thought it was not needed. For tired persons, a bed is more important than a large space! Very quickly, we were dead asleep. Are not we most happy when our senses lay to rest? SâEkhya[25] said our mental and bodily pain sheltered in our senses.

---

[24] *A concept when human beings get graced by their natural endowments.*
[25] *An Indian philosophical system.*

DAY - 3

LAKE, CONFERENCE, FOREST

Tour of Chilika

We got up early and got ready by 5:30 AM. We carried our bags, checked out at the front desk and took the car to the lab. The guard at the gate recognized us and let us in. We parked the car and went behind the building to the dock. Our boat person was already there. We greeted him and he let us ride the boat. It was a motor boat with low roof; one needed to be careful. We stepped in lowering our heads. It was designed for about a dozen people to sit. An assistant to the driver showed up. We started moving.

The sun had not risen; the air was still. It felt a bit chill but crisp. The water looked clean. It had a light blue colour. Occasionally weeds would float by. I touched water stretching my hands down. It was an exhilarating experience. I had never been in open lake waters so close to it in my adult life. I was told that Chilika was shallow. The water depth varied between two feet and eight feet. There was no current, nor were there any hidden rocks.

We saw large areas demarcated with poles. They were special spawning areas leased to fishing contractors. We saw tourist boats with people. Our boatman knew his way. We were proceeding towards *Nalabana*[26]. *Nalabana* is an aquatic weed forest so called because the plants look like tubes, -in Oriya. It was a low-height-island in the lake and special favourite for the migrating birds. The sun was up and tides were in. The water was wavy and the boat splashed water on us. The boat could be making a three-foot excursion up and down. The boatman's assistant negotiated the sides to stabilize the boat. He gave us plastic pads to use as shields against the splashing water.

I was in Chilika to get a feel of the open waters. The coastal areas were in focus those days because of terrorist and drug incursions through the coastlines. It was not easy to detect small boats from space, but one could detect the tracks of motor boats. Technology is developed to distinguish watercolour which is an indication of change in temperature and calcification in the reef areas. Multi-wavelength cameras can watch the oceans high up in the sky and check for the differentials in the water conditions. Chilika looked clean. The visible colour variation in its water was negligible. Its shallowness was a problem because silt could deposit and clog it up. Unchecked fisheries and arbitrary construction of spawning ponds had almost destroyed the lake. There had been efforts to clean the lake during the last few years.

We passed through the rough area and now the water was still again. The boatman declared that we were in *Nalabana*. The weed forest was drowned in the monsoons and he wanted us to imagine the largeness of the space. He parked the boat there by shutting down the engine.

---

[26] *A large pool of tuber like plants shooting from the mud. They serve as food to the fishes and aquatic creatures.*

He used a pole to get weeds from the lake floor. He said that the weeds were nutritious for the fish. Many small organisms grew, lived and died in them. I wondered about my project of finding water in Mars in search of life. It was not clear why water should sustain life, but there was empirical evidence. It was also not clear if life created itself, or if there was a celestial force that came into play. These organisms were winners. Once life forms it can stick around. One day some of these organisms could evolve to become human beings! They would visit to examine other organisms in the lake!

Our friend talked about the fragility of the seaweeds, how susceptible they were to minor variations in water temperature and chemistry. He said it took much effort to clean up the water in the lake. He was happy about the progress. He had been on the job for more than twenty years. He knew the difficulties. We talked about the villages around and their social conditions. He talked about the hardship of communication and food. I saw in him a man of nature. Such men possibly left the Orissa shores in boats to find navigation routes to faraway lands. He was tough; his bones were strong. We treated him with biscuits and fruits that Nagen had carried. The sun was up about twenty degrees; it was getting warm. We had a party in the lake.

Kalijai[27] **Temple**

We reached the *Kalijai* Temple. It was an island inside the lake made famous by the legend of a boat accident caused by the stormy winds in the lake. History said that the deities from the Puri Temple were hidden in the island

---

[27] *A fabled deity commemorating the storm vortices in the lake. There is a folk legend of a bride perishing through a boat accident in a sudden cyclonic storm.*

to protect them against desecration by the invading Muslims. We docked the boat and proceeded towards the temple. It seemed like a modified structure, freshly painted with multiple colours. A former king of a local princely state maintained it. The king ruled over all the neighbourhood villages. There was a young boy as a priest in the Temple. A man outside claimed to be the head priest. The process of calling oneself a priest without formal training in Sanskrit or rituals had started bothering me. I did not understand if it was convenience or if it fought unemployment. The young boy had little to do with the issues of the world. He appeared sincere, but did not care to know why even a *Devi* is conceived to exist!

We participated in a *Puja*[28] in the temple and then went around island. There was a forest like setting with a gravel-stone path bordering the water. We walked the path. Dirty and filthy smell increased. One does notwalk too fast through on a gravel path. People came for picnics and used the area as toilet. It was unhygienic and antisocial. The Government had not developed the area to facilitate enough public bathrooms. The bathroom near the Temple lacked maintenance. Bathroom facilities in India continued to be a huge sanitary issue. Modern plumbing has not reached the villages. India continued to operate in vacuum of public engineering for the last several centuries. Independence has brought factories but has not resolved the basic needs. We pulled ourselves forward. Nagen followed me; occasionally he guided me in negotiating the path. Mali was near the boat looking at the water from the porch.

It was 8:30 AM. The return journey was quick. We passed by the INS Chilika, an Indian Navy outpost in the

---

[28] *A Hindu worship service.*

lake. I had heard shooting noises earlier that I had ignored. They came from the drills in the Naval School. There was a high barbed wire fence around the periphery of the island hosting the school. We proceeded. The waves had died down; the ride was easy. We saw tourist boats returning, they went to a different dock. We saw some debris on water, possibly dumped by the joy-riders. They needed to put stronger public messages and institute a patrol. Conservation is not easy. Nature responds slowly and we kill species. To enjoy nature and leave it unspoiled is a task. India is a paradise of natural resource; they need maintenance. Everybody needs education in conservation and preserving the nature. I recalled the conservation efforts at the massive Yellowstone National Park in the US. Conservation can indeed create natural laboratories.

Coastal Zone Conference

We were guided to attend the Coastal Zone Conference. It was attended by about thirty individuals, six or so visiting out of State. Several NGO's had been active in Chilika work, and were represented. In the morning session, the emphasis was on the nutrient management. We took our seats in the audience. There was a United Nations person of Indian origin from an office in Kenya. He was the lead speaker. A Government of India person followed him on fisheries. Director of Chilika Development Authority spoke next. They brought home the point that the industrialization in Mahanadi delta could cause effluents to drain to the lake. This could do serious harm to the aquatic habitat. The Space Application Centre at Ahmedabad had advised them to use satellite images to monitor the condition of water by checking the watercolour.

There was vigorous discussion about restricting sewer and effluents reaching the lake. Many commented about the inadequacy of enforcement. I stated that seepage of effluents would do damage at the lake floor vegetation. The discoloration at the surface could be noticeable when the organics in the whole water column had been rotted out. My point of view was that the shallowness of the lake would need quicker management time scale than in the open ocean. I suggested that a better way of detecting pollutants could be to track fish migration since the fish would be more sensitive to the toxicity of the effluents. It would need a good study of the fish habitat through careful tracking and long-term observation. Others agreed on this point and said they would proceed to find solutions. I said I would help what I could.

Lunch was served in the Guesthouse and it was well done. We enjoyed discussing issues with the delegates and learned of their interests more. The United Nations person was an economist. He was more concerned with the overall economic gain from the fisheries. I did not have time to learn about the allocation of funds for the resources like Chilika. I found all of them were well meaning and sincere. I was happy. We wanted to move on. We thanked the Director for all the arrangements and we begged leave of all.

We had scheduled to proceed south in the trip and returning to Bhubaneswar through the forest roads. My intention was to visit the birthplace of the Oriya poet Upendra Bhanja. We asked for the road directions. The Chief scientist knew the area; he guided us. It sounded a bit hazy. The directions in India are always a bit vague. We had to explore forward.

On road to Gulunda

Upendra Bhanja[29] is considered the greatest among the Oriya poets in the last three hundred years. His style of writing had impressed me from my High School days. His word skills of doing algebra with the letters were fascinating. While such alphabet acrobatics are uncommon in the world literature, it was a pastime in India. Upendra Bhanja was a master. I was curious about the schooling he might have had to help develop his vocabulary. He must have been extremely skilled in many languages and in music since he wrote his lyric with built in melody. Orissa had a rich repertoire of prosodic styles that the poets used. This was only a few hundred years ago, one feels ashamed that we have so little left of this high cultural tradition. An occupied nation loses her voice!

The areas of southern Chilika and Ganjam had been centers of Oriya arts and literature for a long time. The old Kalingans operated from this area. The land was prosperous. Some people said the true Oriya soul was in Ganjam since their language is clean and clear. Another king from the area called for the dignity of Orissa and the Oriya language not too long ago. I had visited the area as a kid. One of my father's three sisters was married in a lawyer's family in Berhampur. My aunt was a social activist and worked for the women's welfare in the area that had a larger context in the national scene. Her husband was the Public Prosecutor for the district. I would consider him the most affectionate man that lived on earth!

I thought about Ganjam more. My father loved the area. There were leftist strongholds he visited. We would

---

[29]Called *Kavisamrâm*, the emperor among the poets, for his prolific writings and ornamented word plays in poetic compositions.

meet skilled folk singers who would mesmerize audiences with their voice and art. Their knowledge of Oriya literature was superb. Singing with the rhythm of two musically banging sticks held peculiarly through various finger positions was fascinating and entertaining. Called *Dasakathia* in Oriya, the style, the ambience and the power of folk entertainment were impressive. Then there would be another style where a group would present literature analytically while rendering in music. There could be five to seven people in the group, among them some good actors and humourists. The group would perform to present the intricacies of poetic literature for the enjoyment of the people. *Pala* as it is called in Oriya was one of the finest and richest forms of literary exposition invented by man. I had not researched on the origin of these art forms. I learned that these modes of arts were slowly dying away; the new youth is going for service jobs. We need efforts for their preservation.

We turned inward away from Chilika at Khallikote. These areas were inhabited by staunch Oriya nationalists like there existed Marathi nationalists at Pune in Maharashtra. Oriya soldiers and musclemen fought from here against the Moghuls; then against the British. The struggle was similar to Shivaji's covert struggle against Aurangzeb. Oriyas eventually fell, not to Moghuls but to the Marathas. Marathas had horses, Orissa elephants were not deployed properly. The Maratha intruders had better hit and run technique. Oriyas were defensive; did not care to go after others. In wars, offense wins; one has to keep one leg up. As the car moved through the road, the surface became rugged. Gradually it was only dirt. There were very few people on the road; there were patches of slums on the sides. My delirium of Oriya stalwart was slowly evaporating. I saw a starving population. A young man staring at the car with a bike was the only noticeable road scene. I asked Mali to stop the car such that I could speak to the young man.

I softly asked how he was doing. I asked if he knew the road to Gulunda, Bhanja's birthplace. He looked weak. His eyes blank, no shine. He said he was going to a village five miles away. He appeared to lack stamina. He knew the area though. On the second question, he said we should take a right turn at the next intersection. I wanted to talk to him more but we were not ready. We were more eager to reach the destination. Time was short. We reached the intersection as the man had indicated. We saw a public transport bus standing on the road. The bus was dusty and crowded. It could be the only conveyance for many in the area to go out somewhere. The bus I saw was a relic of the early days. It seemed to be parked for some time. The schedule of transport was determined by allowing people to gather. No transport might show up until the next day. Not much had changed in forty years since I last took that bus!

We took the turn and moved. Now we discovered that the road was dug up and there was no diversion. Mali looked at me if we should proceed. We had no choice, we had to move. He tried. We went slowly. It was bumpy, bad for the car. I felt guilty that I subjected others to this exercise. The stretch continued for about twenty miles with intermittent variations. No contractor or any worker was on the scene. It was not clear to imagine what might have happened. The area with bumps and boulder could pass as Martian highlands! We proceeded with the lethargy of a Mars rover except we were time bound and we were on earth. Later I heard that the Government was too busy around Bhubaneswar and there was little development elsewhere. It was new kind of oppression on people!

We reached another intersection and asked a group of people standing on the side. They said we were still forty kilometres away, but the road would be better. They seemed to be of forgiving type. They did not complain that they did not deserve those conditions. Nothing better was seen. Bhubaneswar was another continent away. In an earlier discussion in my home, Nagen had concluded that Oriyas were tolerant and of accepting type. I saw that in the field. I had heard that anger could build up, not because of poor transportation but because there was no administration. There were no offices, no police, no building, no school; no place to sit. Some paddy fields and forests were at the distance, beautiful but lonely. I had difficulty understanding the neglect. Mali said that Government was giving subsidized rice at two rupees a kilogram, and that made people lazy. I countered that there was no work anyway, no investment of any kind. The whole area slept. Mali said some woke up in the night to kidnap and abduct!

We reached Gulunda. The market and stores were lined for quarter of a mile. There was nothing obvious about the famous poet on the road. We asked, and got direction to a store that helped in the local celebration of Bhanja's birth anniversary in spring. People there advised us to go up the hill to the *Bagiswari*[30] Temple to see the statue. We trekked up. The scenery looked spectacular up there. We saw the statue of the famous poet in the courtyard. A handsome man, a pair of moustache adored his face; the eyes were sweet. I was seeing freedom and

---

[30]*Another incarnation of the Devî.*

passion in his soul. Poets are always romantic. This person knew his words. He knew how words can charm the readers. We lingered there several minutes. He wrote his creations at this temple. This was his home. The palace people had thrown him out. Who wants a poet in house?

The shrine was locked. We viewed the deity through the door. We prayed for grace. We bowed. Creative work is an experience; some higher power must protect us, give us brains and skills. Words just do not crop up; nobody has understood how we think. First, we think; then we render to understandable words. People read when the words are good. All readers know what is good, but a writer may not know what is good. An unseen external power does the quality check; the poet is a medium. Sarala[31] knew it, Kalidasa[32] had the diction, Valmiki[33] had originally perfected it. Some people think Bhanja's creations are erotic. Eroticism is in the mind of the reader not in the literature. The poet enjoys the words rendered; the universe speaks through the poet. Creativity manifests through passion.

A locked building next to the Temple served as the local library. The surrounding did not look clean. The volunteers might not be poets. Orderliness is the first characteristic of a poet. Let it be simple, it should be orderly. The universe has an order; the poets celebrate order. It is called *vAk*; it is an old concept. *vAk* has no sound, it is the stillness of the mind, it is the search and curiosity. Thought shows up, words follow. It is feminine

---

[31] *Sarala Das, the famed Oriya poet of fifteenth century, known as the father of the modern Oriya literature.*
[32] *The famous Sanskrit poet of fourth century.*
[33] *The author of epic Ramayana of first century.*

in concept; it is nurturing in its attribute. It covers itself in colorless white and likes clean locations. We worship her as the deity Saraswati[34]; here she is Bagiswari.

Dasapalla, Nayagarh

We were back in the market. I looked for some fruits; there was none. I guessed Nayagarh should be nearby and I had thought we should halt there for an evening walk. We saw a sign to Dasapalla and decided to take the road. The road was single lane but good. We had entered the famous Dasapalla kingdom where I wanted to come during my father's electioneering. We did not see any traffic on the road. Occasionally the village women walked with twig bundles on their head. A massive herd of cows came by. Big bodies dwarfed the tiny car. The scene reminded me of bison herds in Yellowstone. Cows have bigger eyes; they look at you. Bisons have drooped eyes; they mostly look down. We were told that the bisons were dangerous because they get upset if someone blocked them. The cows crowded around the car, but moved forward. Unlike the bisons they did not look through the window glass. A big relief!

We had entered the forest. We saw signs for "elephants crossing the road". It got exciting. We were not ready to confront a herd of elephants! I did not know if anyone else was reading the signs. I realized that such adventure needed caution. We were unprepared. Nobody warned us before. Though I would love to see an elephant herd, I wished they did not show up. I keenly watched both sides. Mali was concentrating on the road. Nagen might be already thinking that I was too crazy. He was our only resource if

---

[34]*The Hindu Goddess of speech and knowledge.*

something went wrong. I did not have the courage to break the silence. There was a sense of nervousness in travelling this winding and never-ending road. We wanted to escape before it was dark.

We saw a sign for Dasapalla town. We reached an intersection and we had to choose between Nayagrah and Dasapalla towns. It was 8 PM; we had to move forward. We chose Nayagarah line. We were on a State highway, two-lane road connecting the western Orissa to Bhubaneswar. Trucks were showing up and the traffic had to be negotiated. We reached a well-lighted area and we thought it was Nayagarh. I did not see the familiar landscape that I had in memory. I kept the thoughts to myself. With my immature planning, I had thought to be in Cuttack in the evening for a meeting with my old friends from Ravenshaw Collegiate School. I called Cuttack and they said that they had assembled and were waiting. I did not tell them that I was in a different planet. You do not crack humour when you are guilty! My friend Saroj recommended that travel to Cuttack late night would not be safe and requested me to abandon the idea. Safety on the roads was a new concern in travel. Law and order do take a tailspin through institutional corruption.

There were some summer festivities going on, shops had been set up. We parked the car some distance away from the market area. The place looked like the Fair scenes in the interior US except there was a visible police presence. We returned to search for some food. Nayagarh cheesecake[35] was famous and I searched for the store.

---

[35] *An Oriya sweet made by baking organically wrapped cheese in a charcoal oven.*

They said actual Nayagarh market was further down and we should explore there. We had no patience to wait. We took some locally made fried snacks and shared among ourselves.

I kept wondering why the roads were bad. I would have examined outside had it been daytime. Was it engineering or was it pure usurping the funds? The area looked uncared for. Where did the money go? It was confusing. I understood there were representatives in the State assembly and they fought for various causes every day. Why could not they fight for good roads? Was it all connected? Where were the people? Was all energy sapped out? People in this land fought against oppression, why were they hiding? I could not discuss any of these in a running car. I did not wish to cause distraction. The disturbances stayed inside, they simmered. I saw my own mind wanderings here; one had to hold it through yoga.

Khurdha neared and we saw some lights. Road widened, we had come to a two-lane road; it was the National Highway. I was relieved to see activity around. It was nothing like factories and manufacturing plants one saw in other areas of the country, but some chimneys oozing smoke in smelting shops. We proceeded. Bhubaneswar neared. I suggested to my friends if we should sit down in a restaurant to refresh ourselves to disengage from the road. Both Mali and Nagen said that they wanted to go home. They were eager to reach home. I was not clear about my meal. Nobody was waiting for me; I was the only person accountable for my own adventure. The pleasure of sharing the day's story to a willing listener is a luxury for human beings. My mother was a willing listener of travel stories. Now all are busy, everything is trivial unless there is overlapping common interest. Instead of telling, I might write later. I wondered about the need of a mother in the universe.

We dropped off Nagen first; he said he would pick up his transport the next day. Mali dropped me off at my sister's house. The house was crowded; there had been many new arrivals. All of them were busy in a side room doing some massive textile distribution. It is an old wedding ritual; the close relatives were given dresses. I have not understood the significance of the dress distribution; possibly, it represented the glory of the local product. I let go. My sister served me some food. I ate and took rest. It was close to midnight.

DAY-4

BHUBANESWAR

Prachi[36] River Valley

I am an early riser. Here I was in an open room in a different bed. I was up at 4 AM; I lingered such that I did not disturb others. I did not know when others slept. About 5 AM or so, I thought of brushing my teeth and taking a wash. It is not always easy to find one's way in a new place. I navigated my way in the dark and succeeded. I was out, everyone was still sleeping. I sat down on the sofa and tried to look up the newspaper on the table. The news content in the local newspaper was not very appealing. I had further difficulty with the artificiality of expression. Lately I learned that the newspaper staff did collect their news cable in English and translate to the local language by using a language dictionary. The product was rushed and had very little quality control. The person translating would lack proficiency in the language. There was little time for revision. The language read distorted. The readers have to accept. The emphasis and the melody of the language got

---

[36] *A branch of Kathjodi river in Mahanadi river delta.*

lost. Some people commented, but the protest was timid. I learned that it has happened in almost all vernacular newspapers in India. Decay of nativity is the continued outcome of the colonial rule!

Laxmi, my old friend from MIT, had scheduled a trip to visit some of the newly discovered archaeological ruins in some local rural areas. He had a friend who had been interested in the upkeep of the heritage. The friend had explored and recovered many old ruins. Forest brush covered up unused temples. The friend made efforts to mobilize volunteers to clear the brush and check. Marvellous stone deities got buried inside. He had brought to light many pieces of exquisite art. These ruins were on the banks of Prachi River, a branch of Mahanadi in its delta. Prachi River banks are famous for many old established temples that Oriyas use for worship and pilgrimage. A lot of history is hidden in the area. It is the old Oriya land.

Laxmi showed up at 7:30 in a full-size Toyota van. His brother-in-law would accompany us. Prabhat was a journalist and a writer; he kept interest in Orissa and her heritage. It was a good company. We proceeded. We would go to a village called Adasapur where we would meet Hansanath, the friend archaeologist who would escort us to the ruins. Things appeared to go like clockwork thanks to the communications through the new convenience of mobile phone. A person in a Gandhian dress of a homespun kurta, dhoti and a bag on his right shoulder greeted us on the road. This happened suddenly in a crowded market area. It appeared like a space rendezvous. It was about 9 AM. He got in the car. He complained that we were late and we must rush. Laxmi introduced him to all. We stopped in another market area further down. We took some fruits and tea. We kept moving.

We were going into the land of *Madhava*[37], a cult developed in Orissa in the seventh century. It was the time when *Shakti* worship was dominating at Banapur that I visited two days ago. Prachi was the northern fringe of that kingdom. *Madhava* is Sri Krishna but why he is worshipped as *Madhava* is unknown to me. Sarala Dasa wrote that Lord Vishnu disguised himself in the forest when *Kali*[38] age arrived after Sri Krishna's death. This disguise was in the form of a rock that eventually took a bluish hue by aging and vegetation. The locals believed it to be an animated object and offered worship to it. This became the legend of *Nilamadhava*. Eventually a king came in search of the deity and through various tribulations installed the deity as the wood-carved icons in the newly built Puri Temple. Sarala Dasa was a magnificent storyteller; everything he said would appear realistic. He designed stories, he made up most of them in his efforts of bringing the epics to the masses. He had his own imagination of Mahabharata, Sri Krishna and Orissa. He was the king among the myth-makers. We had to also think how much myth was hidden in the epics themselves!

Poet Jayadeva wrote poems about *Madhava*. The poet's birthplace is nearby. Oriyas did not know that Jayadeva was taken over by the Bengalis for a long time. It was quite possible that Jayadeva migrated to Orissa. *Madhava* is the key; there was no *Madhava* anywhere else besides this little stretch on earth. Jayadeva was a melodious poet, possibly also a singer. His *Madhava* was sensuous, a divinity who wanted to live with the mortals.

---

[37] *A deity associated with Sri Krishna, old in origin.*
[38] *Hindus believe in cyclic evolution of time divided in four segments. The last segment (current) is Kali.*

There was an attractive force between the deity and the humanity as with two opposite poles. The making of Radha[39] and making of the concept of dual-divinity was Jayadeva's art. To write devotional love as amorous poetry needed passion and musicality. Jayadeva tapped into it and produced the loveliest love songs offered as the play of polarities, a male and a female. His composition was in twelfth century AD. The ruins we were visiting are of eighth or ninth century AD.

We took turn to a village road; it was concrete, about six feet wide and six inches thick. It looked out of place for the village, but was interesting. Laxmi said that it was the initiative of the Prime Minister Manmohan Singh that all villages should have good roads. It was not clear why they forgot the villages in the southern Orissa. The concrete road led us to a forty feet high temple. We parked the van and entered the gate. The priest showed us the deity with a clay lamp, the carving was exquisite. The stone was polished granite. I could feel the care to the details. I appreciated the artistry. The deity was about three feet high. It was *Basudeva Madhava*; the temple was Bhaskareswara. There was a huge Shiva[40] Linga[41] worshipped on a side. The priest let us offer worship there. Then we noticed a magnificent Garuda[42] statue in black granite. Garuda is the mythical bird that flies like an eagle. In Hindu mythology, it is taken as the transport for Lord Vishnu. The Garuda that we were seeing had a high nose human face, sharp in its features, strong in its body. It was more than two feet

---

[39] *Consort of Sri Krishna, considered an artificial construct by the poet Jayadeva.*
[40] *The third of the Hindu Trinity.*
[41] *An iconic rock signature appearing like a phallic symbol.*
[42] *An eagle-like bird that helps transport the Hindu god Vishnu.*

high. Hansanath told us that it was one of the largest Garuda statues in the area. I admired the artistry, the creativity, and the sheer beauty of the visual.

We proceeded to another Temple; I do not remember the name. Here we saw an eighteen-arm *Shakti* idol with some Buddhist icons under the base. Hansanath said that the deity depicted the victory of *Shakti* against the Buddhism. I did not ask how he knew. Interpretation of Indian iconography is rampant in the west, and various theories prop up. Speculations become knowledge. Indians lack time and opportunity to interpret what the objects meant, they just exist. Texts, material and literature are hidden in places. The foreigners discovered mostly accidentally. There was a new awakening among some in the country. To understand India's history objectively was another matter. Most were written in a hand-waving manner in the pre-independence days. It was not easy to question something that has been provided as education. India's freedom was not complete yet. Some jingoists and people in politics shouted hollow slogans. We need serious scholarship by people who lived in the country. I told Hansanath to dig in through his research and discover new things. I also suggested to keep an open mind about everything and not to assume anything. It would need work. True India must reveal herself!

We continued our expedition. More temples came; more carvings, more beauty. Sometimes it was *Madhava*, sometimes it was *Shakti*, some other times it was a *Linga*. Sometimes the temple exterior would be simple and some other time the exterior would have elaborate carvings like those in the temples at Bhubaneswar. Private individuals were responsible in building these monuments. Who were those artistic philanthropists? I reflected on the artisans.

Who were they? How did they disappear? Thought came that the carving could be a pastime, an artistic expression. People were trying to compose their thoughts on stone. It was not clear how much time was spent in carving the object. I loved the clean lines and the fine ridges. It was the poet Kalidasa writing on stone; free, creative and detailed!

We reached the Baraha Temple. It was a National Heritage Site, possibly one of a kind of such temple in the world. Baraha, the boar, is the third incarnation of Vishnu. The boar pulled the earth out from the deluge that is believed to happen when the creation suspends itself for a while. Again, a beautiful creation in art, some non-believer would certainly be disturbed. Why celebrate a boar! It is a well-maintained Temple with good gardens around. I loved the setting and the iconography. It was good that the Temple was deep inside the valley, not easily reachable unless one knew the area. There is alarming idol destruction in the world!

The sun was hot; the concrete was capturing heat. Hansanath reminded that it was one o'clock and we should return to another village for lunch. There were no navigation markings on the road, there was confusion which way to go. We proceeded in right direction. We crossed a bridge, possibly a hundred feet long. He told that we had crossed Prachi River five times during our excursion. We reached our destination temple where people were waiting for us. It was another *Madhava* Temple. We went around the shrine and came to the front porch. The lunch was ready. We washed our face and sat down. The food was simple. Rice was of a different type, sweeter. They had a special lentil with boiled vegetables that every Oriya loves. Then there was a dish of mixed vegetable, and sweet chutney. Given my restrictions on outside food, I needed to be careful in these interior areas. The ground water was used from a well and I felt comfortable. It was a good intimate lunch. There was more discussion on *Madhava* and the artistic heritage of Prachi valley. I would like to talk to someone who came from the local carver family. Everything takes time. Time was not in our favour.

Reading *Saptauati*[43] in Bhubaneswar

We had to return. I had scheduled with Gita and Nagen to commence a Devi reading at a Temple in Bhubaneswar at 3 PM. This was a family meeting for my brother. Our other cousins and friends in Bhubaneswar would join. I requested people to keep moving. We reached the outskirts of Bhubaneswar. The town was spread out and there was late afternoon traffic. They dropped me off at my sister's house about 4 PM. I changed over to Indian style dress to prepare myself for sitting on the floor for several hours. I took my books, hired a rickshaw. Guided by Nagen on the phone I shot forward to Gita's house. After passing through the ridges and valleys on the side road I reached the house. It was a delight; a solo accomplishment! We walked to the local *Mangala*[44] Temple where the Devi reading was scheduled. It was not very far. It was a neatly kept Temple with a spacious courtyard. The priest asked us to use the porch in front of the main shrine. We settled down with our books. I kept a cup of water to protect my throat from drying up in heat. It would take us three hours to complete the reading.

---

[43] *A book of seven hundred verses extolling the power of the Devi on the earth.*
[44] *A representation of Devi from a scriptural angle.*

Devi Mahatmya comes from the Sanskrit literary epic Markandeya Purana. I have not done much research about the personality of Markandeya. I gather that he was a prominent sage in the old days and wrote many useful compositions. *Devi Mahatmya* is also called *Durga Saptasati*, seven hundred stanzas offered to Goddess Durga. It is the most popular *Shakta* text extolling the reign of the feminine spirit in the universe. Our arrogance and our humility- both originate in the feminine nature. The book enunciates the sustenance of the universe with a grace of a Divine Mother who incarnates herself in various forms to protect the humanity. Arrogance and blind ambition are the part of engineering in the design of the universe and we need a Mother to bring discipline and peace. Her grace gives us food and health. We call her attention to our woes since she could be busy in doing things elsewhere assisting someone else!

I started reading, Nagen joined. A mother and daughter team from the local Sri Aurobindo Society showed up. My sister Apu and her husband showed up after an hour. Some other people gathered and we gave them books to read. Suddenly a local devotee in the Temple started reciting the stanzas before I read. It became a distraction. I suggested to him that we do the reading in sequence; he did not agree and left. In the Devi theory, it is all Devi's play. You do not know why what may happen. You just accept; you cannot do anything different. We continued; the congregation increased. Various other people joined in. The final parts of reading were beautiful and sweet. We read them together in resonance; the sound was interesting. Everyone's voice was bold and convincing. After we finished, I asked people to offer songs and prayers. Some volunteered. Not everybody is prepared for a temple ritual. It could be a function of one's own upbringing.

The priest helped us wrap up with a final worship. A massive percussion group assembled for the 7 PM *Arati*[45]. There was thumping of cymbals, drums, sticks and bells. These are Devi's instruments, primitive and simple. She has been in the universe before anyone else existed. Her sound begins with a conch. We offered fruits and light to the deity. Everybody was in a devotional mood. We ended our reading in obeisance.

Gita had arranged *Mahaprasada*[46] from the famous Lingaraja[47] temple. *Mahaprasada* food is specially cooked from fresh ingredients following strict ritualistic rules. The taste is delicious. Many of our cousins and relatives living in Bhubaneswar area had shown up. Gita's sisters and their families were also there. It was a large family get-together. Everybody sat on the courtyard floor. Food was served on specially made leaf plates. I enjoyed the gathering and enjoyed the food. Group eating is an old Oriya tradition. Oriya food preparation is different from other areas. The spices were half-ground; one senses it. Vegetables were plentiful; the rice was special and different. We finished our food, washed our hands. There were a lot of jokes and pleasantries going around. It was a pleasant evening. Family reunions are always special. Apu brought me back to my place of stay. I rested for the night.

---

[45] *The hymnal service for the presiding deity.*
[46] *Specially cooked food sanctified by religious offerings in a Temple.*
[47] *The famous Shiva temple in Bhubaneswar of eleventh century.*

DAY-5

BHUBANESWAR

Wedding Preparation

My sister's house was crowded now. Her husband Anjan was the ninth among ten siblings. His father had two other brothers; together Anjan's family has twenty-five cousins from the three brothers. Most have shown up. I lost count on the names and the origin. Anjan's eldest sister has been a friend to me. She briefed me occasionally as the congregation evolved. People came from Baripada, a town about a hundred and fifty miles north from Bhubaneswar. Baripada was an old princely kingdom, known for its progressive king. It had given freedom to women before it became a buzz in the rest of the country. King of Baripada made much philanthropy towards the higher education in Orissa.

I saw the dominance of women belonging to Baripada in the current household. Everyone had come to help Anjan in his first major social obligation. Men existed, but they quickly disappeared. The language was northern Oriya; a dialect spoken by prolonging the vowels. I liked the sound. Women appeared busy, moving from one room to the other briskly. Apparently, huge organizational work had to be accomplished. I was not very familiar with how weddings are done. Each of the new arrivals appeared to know his or her move. His move was to keep away or work outside; her move was to check the quality of work and pitch in wherever needed. Such activities possibly have happened before, all seemed to have experience. My friend, the eldest sister in the group, was the leader. She directed the operation and guided the traffic.

Indian weddings continue to maintain their old origin. The bride's family would arrange objects such that everything would look elegant and beautiful; the groom's family would show up with a whole platoon of people to be feted as respected guests. The groom's family had upper hand; they could walk out any time on their whim. The bride's family had to be careful such that no discomfort is complained about. In olden times, there was valour involved; the groom had to exhibit that he deserved the girl. Valmiki had institutionalized this through Sita's[48] wedding. In the current times, the valour was replaced with gaudy dress and unusual props adding showmanship to the process. In the new immigrant societies, abroad, the groom could show up on a horse back in a hotel lobby. It is a spectacle to confuse the hotel guests. If no horse, loud music through a DJ and arbitrary dancing could simulate the spirit of jubilation. Consumerism and business interests have replaced the solemnity of betrothal.

The massive organization was to create scores of packages that would be given as gifts to the relatives who show up. Each person of the groom's party received a gift package. All packages needed be assembled and wrapped.

---

[48] *The consort of Rama in the epic Ramayana.*

An elder woman had brought hundreds of packages of a candy of a lentil sweet from Baripada. It was unique to the area. It had nice colour and good texture; was made with lentil flour, butter and sugar. It has longer shelf life than the wet sweets used in lower Orissa. I tasted a piece; it was good and chewy. To accompany it, they had a large supply of hot-mix added in each package. The snack added the native touch to the event. The groom's party could munch on it during their journey back home.

My guide sister briefed me that the hot-mix added to puffed rice made a great snack. It was among the staple food in Baripada. I had heard the love of puffed rice to Baripada before; now I was hearing from a person who lived it. Once she told the story, the entire team of sisters and brothers pitched in and told about the significance of puffed rice as food: "it was unique and versatile"; "it mixed well with the vegetables, lentils and meat in a thousand ways". I heard proud and satisfied voices. They would say in unison that it was the most savoury dish for a person from Baripada. Each person now held a bowl of puffed rice with hot-mix as his or her breakfast. There was a chorus of request if I would join them. I agreed to join the community ritual. To consume a bowl of puffed rice can take any length of time. I thought it was a way to hold people together unlike the quick breakfast we do abroad. My sister seemed perfectly in tune to the ritual. Even the younger college-going daughter joined in with a bowl.

Lakhi's house has a nice spacious balcony that she has decorated with flower pots. Streams of colorful lights were hanging from the roof and they announced the festivity in the evening. The balcony served as my office during my stay. I used the telephone, read newspapers. I met friends. Some of the men in the family came by and discussed about life abroad. A couple was interested in space missions. We discussed possible extra-terrestrial life.

I needed to get ready for the day. I had to go to the bank to cash some traveller's checks and visit Sanjoy on the way. In the evening, I had to attend a meeting arranged by Laxmi at an Industrial Park in the outskirts of the city.

Visit to Sanjoy

The road to Sanjoy's apartment was getting familiar to me now though there was no known street address. The organization of the layout was through regions. In the regions, there would be various blocks of buildings as anchors. One went forward, backward, or sideways from such buildings. In conversations, people nodded their head claiming to know the intricate details involved. I knew such in Cuttack during my teenage years. One must walk or bike the roads many times a week for the scenes to sink in. There was an ownership to such knowledge. It was a cartographic map in the person's head. It could unravel in need. A stranger would get lost; he would be easily detected in the neighbourhood.

I hired a rickshaw and got the driver connected to Gita to get the directions. Things happened in regular manner. The Khyber Pass showed up. I held the railings tight and overcame the peril. Thought had come if the rickshaw would overturn in one of those brown ditches. Being in space-related work, I did not think the probability would be zero. I just wished that the event must not happen. The ditches were there to test human determination and perseverance amidst the mud of the society. The rickshaw entered the higher ground and then turned. There was the familiar white-colour one-storey house. I paid the fare, knocked the door and walked in.

The nurse's aide asked me to wash my hands before I entered Sanjoy's room. My emotional hugging on the first day did not go well with my brother's low tolerance to infection. He coughed in the night. There must not be any dust in the room. I complied and washed my hands. There was a television set in the room broadcasting music. Sanjoy was looking. His eyes had a constant gaze; his lips showed movement. Sometimes his body would vibrate. It could be interpreted as laughter. I went near him and tried to speak to him. Normally he would understand me completely. Now he looked to me with still eyes. His cognitive faculties were returning; his response in eyes was my test. I had done work on brain earlier when I wanted to understand the mechanics of the mind. Now I was seeing the evidence that the body and mind were indeed separate. The mind might understand, but would not manifest in the body. It was a function of neurological system triggering the muscle system through blood flow. There could be a delay and there are loops. Cognitive reaction of muscles is the signature of life. I thought of Norbert Wiener and the theory of threshold and feedback. I remained unsettled.

Visit to Bank

It was time to go to the Bank. I had an account at the United Commercial Bank in the Market Building. I hired a rickshaw and proceeded. The market area had expanded; new buildings had come up. There were garment stores and shoe stores, small convenience stores, utensil stores, tool stores; all in ten foot by ten foot cabins. The structures looked temporary, but possibly had been standing for years. I recognized the main market building and there was a gate. I had heard that the market building was a planned construction like the entire city. The population projection was incorrect; nothing looked like having an order or a design.

I found my way to the Bank and checked if I could cash some traveller's checks. The clerk told that the network was down and there was no link to know the currency rates; the job could not be done. He recommended me to go to the State Bank of India office on the other side of the road. I returned; took a rickshaw requesting to take me to the destination. The rickshaw driver manoeuvred his way around in the back and surfaced himself on the main road. Then it suddenly cut traffic without any signs or alerts. In a flash, we were at the entrance to the State Bank building. The driver veered the vehicle to get the grip on the best surface. The area dropped from the road about five feet. The descent had folds done by water channels. The reverse processing of such channels in Mars has suggested the presence of water there. In the present condition, the water could be real; the traffic was dangerous. My driver was excellent; he did not bother about the small details! He was focused to take me to the front of the building and he did. A frightened man got down from the transport!

I entered the main floor. The foreign exchange section was on the mezzanine. It was tricky to get there; the elevator bypassed the floor. One could only go by the stairs. I negotiated my way. There was a door with a sign 'NRI cell.'[49] Non-Resident Indian is a venerable object in India. Many in Kerala, Gujarat, Punjab and Karnataka channel massive amounts of money to the country. Lately I heard that there was a parallel economy of black money in India. Such

---

[49]*People of Indian origin staying abroad are labelled as NRI. They are assumed to have a higher wealth value.*

money operations were possibly global and various warlords operate militia through such money. It had produced its effect in India. People living abroad from Orissa were not a large number. If I was an example, the dispatch volume was low. I was at the lower end any way; some others were more ambitious. Oriyas in general lacked the income generating capacity, and had not found a niche to create mutual support to develop strength.

Indian rupee is a fluctuating currency. At the time of my first trip in 1972, seven and a half rupees converted to a dollar. The exchange rate to dollar hovered around ten rupees for a long time until there was a gold reserve crisis in 1988. I do not know how it happened, but there was panic in Indian government circles. The currency was devalued.

I entered the NRI room; it was air-conditioned. The room was nicely panelled. There were various bundles of paper stacked in different places. Cabinets existed, but the papers were scattered outside. It was possible that one reached the papers more conveniently if they were outside. A laid-back officer greeted me. I told my need to cash traveller's checks. He said the person at the next desk would help me. The person there was busy in negotiating with another person who was trying to get foreign exchange to make a trip to visit his son. We are always extra cautious when we take our first trip. We think everything is important and give extra attention to trivialities. There is little guidance; each person discovers the path his or her way. Seminars by Banks or Travel Agencies would be an immeasurable help to the first-time travellers.

The officer verified my passport and the visa papers. The exchange rate for the day was somewhere around fifty-five rupees to a dollar. The rupee continued to devalue.

Lately the dollar was also devalued to help boost the US economy. The world economy had suffered terribly with the threats of terrorism and the resultant wars. Some shrewd businesspersons had taken advantage of the situation alluring people to invest in non-existing speculative products. This was a process of pure cheating, but nobody called it so. In most cases, people in power were the beneficiaries and they protect the guilty. The public was busy in maintaining daily life and had no choice but to put its trust in people in power. Sometimes public punishes people in power through the vote and new people quickly tune themselves to the benefits of power. Human greed has its own way to express itself.

The officer asked me about the life abroad. There is always a thought that others' spaces could be better than one's own. I advised him that we had to build our own space by being diligent on everything we do. He expressed his concern on the lack of vernacular education in schools; I agreed with his observation. Language is the channel for human thinking. We can express in any language, but our inner core speaks in our native language. Our views, our personality, our interaction – all are guided by the values we learn in our home through our language. Oriyas by tradition are expected to be gifted artists; the artistry develops through the language that breathes the local air, nurtures itself with the local water. All species know their habitat; we cannot be good human beings unless we feel the power of our birth soil.

Anjan called to arrange to pick me up. I got ready and went outside to wait for my ride.

Meeting at Technology Park

The activity in my sister's house was increasing in

geometric manner. A *shamiana*⁵⁰ had covered the roof and there was a community kitchen there. I took a light lunch. I met many other new people, many new youngsters. There was mirth and noise in the air; it was a massive reunion. The bride herself would show up in the late afternoon, everyone was waiting. She would be taking a train from Calcutta. She was employed there, and lived with friends.

I rested a bit; this was my usual late night time in the US. I still felt dizzy about 3 PM in the afternoon. The event in the evening was being organized by a new NGO⁵¹ called Research and Development Solutions of India. Laxmi was its principal mover; it was made with the support of the local Faculty and scientists. It acted as a think tank. Its goal was to find solutions to local problems. The organization was a year old. Laxmi had briefed me about the increase in depression and mental disorder in India and wanted me to talk about possible remedies using yoga techniques. I had given *"yoga vijñāna"* (the science of yoga) as a title to my talk. I needed to compose my presentation.

Yoga as a technique and philosophy was not so popular in my childhood. I had an uncle, my mother's immediate younger brother who was into naturopathy and yoga exercises. His drinking water through the nostrils was a spectacle for me as a kid. In course of time, I gravitated towards him. He being a science and mathematics teacher, we had mutual liking to each other. In 1963, India celebrated the centenary of Swami Vivekananda's birth and there were all kinds of events. My uncle had a large library of Vivekananda books and the Ramakrishna literature. I

---

⁵⁰*A waterproof canopy with special borders.*
⁵¹*Non-Government Organization – registered public social service organizations working for the community.*

loved them and read most of them through. I also had the goal to prepare for the State competitions on behalf of our school; I won those. Swami Vivekananda's message that we have to respect humanity bore sharpness in its wording and strength in its appeal. I admired the man; the episode that he was transformed by a physical touch by Sri Ramakrishna does continue to remain a puzzle to me till today.

I did not read the Bhagavadgita until I was about 21. I picked up the book with the commentary by Sri Aurobindo from a Sarbodaya book-stall at Nagpur Railway Station. The book was revealing; I loved every line of it. It was the best book I ever read until I read Throreau's Walden. The question of duty and how we perform it had been a source of confusion to me. Do duties show up, or do we choose them? Should we control them? Can we avoid them? The message that one can never control the result was a ringing bell to me. We would try; we could fail. The joy was in trying. Try with your full energy, with your full heart. Let the world figure out success or failure. The performer need not wait for it. It was a difficult but powerful concept. There is no I; it is all we. I gained if the world gained; where was the loss? "We" is large. The larger world we envision, happier we are!

Thirty years later, I had gone to Dwaraka[52] to check on Sri Krishna if the man lived. I came back with a positive answer and shared it with a monk in MIT, Swami Sarvagatananda of Ramakrishna Mission in Boston. He said that not only Sri Krishna lived, but also, he knew what Sri Krishna said. He requested me to collaborate with him to

---

[52] *A town in the west coast of India, reputedly containing the palace of Sri Krishna. Archaeological work is currently underway.*

do the book Sri Krishna Yoga that he had in his mind. It took me five years to produce a hundred-page book. We published it through the Advaita Press in India. Sri Krishna enunciated a doctrine that advised to make sure that all your decisions are done with your full discrimination. Never have an expectation, and do not think you are the doer. While in action keep the mind on it without any stray thoughts. A big prescription, he tried in his life. It is doable but needs massive discipline. He called it yoga. Then we proceeded to do interpretation of Patanjali's Yogasutram[53]; the two volumes Meditation for Spiritual Culmination came out just before the Swami passed away in 2009. Patanjali was a psychologist. To declare that we do not think through our mind was a stroke of genius. Mind is a tool that enhances a thought, he showed by procedures. Then where does the thought come from? What makes us depressed? It gets complicated.

A yogi named Dr. V S Rao had shown up in Boston in 1983 and he discovered me in the Sunday school I helped run for the immigrant children of Indian descent. He had retired from a bank job in Andhra Pradesh[54] and his wife had died. He was a Sanskrit scholar and a yoga instructor. In those days of the early '80s, meditation as a therapy was slowly coming in to the medical fields to help in most difficult cardiac cases. The general population was inflicted with the lavish operations of Mahesh Yogi[55] and the street chanting of Hare Krishna[56]. Many bearded gurus

---
[53] The text enunciating the practice and the philosophy of yoga, dated to first century AD.
[54] A state in the east coast of India.
[55] The Hindu spiritual scholar who propagated yoga through his disciples in the west.
[56] A chant movement initiated in the west by another spiritual teacher Srila Prabhupada from India.

were showing up to share knowledge and earn some money. Dr. Rao appeared different. He was simple, he had no vanity. He started offering yoga classes in our school free of charge. By observing him, I thought he was a good medium to promote the Indian method among the general public.

We would go around to the hospitals, libraries and schools to conduct classes and explain yoga. Simple yoga exercises and techniques of breathing became immense help to many. Such healing was unknown in the US, people showed interest. Many students showed up and they adopted yoga as their profession. We had a movement. I had to keep up with my Sanskrit to read texts to be able to understand and analyse. That the control of life is inside of us needs be experimented; it is a challenge. We met many individuals with various ailments, and quite a few benefited. Dr. Rao passed away in 2007. I was stuck with the question why yoga should heal.

Yoga does not heal; we heal ourselves. Yoga counsels to make the mind silent, the pain could go. How do you make the mind silent? Why is there addiction? Why do we repeat the same mistakes? It is the loneliness and insecurity in life. We depend on others and they betray. We begin to lose confidence in ourselves. Sometimes we ourselves do crooked things, the misdeeds haunt us. How do we give confidence to someone? How do we take away negative thoughts from a person's head? It is a treatment of making one feel good; we can offer friendship; we can hold hands; we can share food. The greatest attribute that man has developed is the attribute of friendship. It does not cost anything; it exists, we manifest. Sometimes we fail to give because we might not have experienced it. That is where yoga comes in. By practicing yogic techniques, we gain confidence that we can help. The rest is a journey.

Nagen showed up, he was my escort to the meeting site. We hired a rickshaw and proceeded towards Khandagiri[57]. We passed by the Raj Bhavan, the official residence of the Governor. The road was winding and we passed by the famous Khandagiri and Udayagiri[58] caves. We stopped by a tea stall and asked people about the Technology Park. None of the assembled people knew. Someone said to go back. There were trees everywhere; there was no sign of any institution. We checked again with a teacher-like person and he directed us to a road. We did reach a gate with the sign that said Biju Patnaik Technology Park. It was about one and half-acre area of green somewhat well kept. There were demonstrations of solar cells and wind turbines. There were various bulletin boards enunciating the energy cycle of the earth. The use of language appeared casual. It could be an effort in public education, which I admired. We were told that we needed to go to the Auditorium that was on the rear side. A middle-aged person there greeted us and escorted us in.

A National Geographic movie on Climate Change was being shown and there were fifty or so high school age girls in the audience. The movie continued for twenty more minutes. The earth was warming, carbon dioxide level was increasing, the glaciers in the North Pole were melting; good stuff to think for the welfare of the planet. I thought there should be a teacher to take questions from the students. It did not happen; the girls filed out after the movie. They were quiet; it appeared as a trip to go out

---

[57]*Caves used as Jaina monasteries and residences, dated to second century BC.*
[58]*The neighbouring hill to Khandagiri, known for architectural ruins.*

than a trip for education. The desired impact of the movie did not seem to register. This was the first time I saw the movie with some High School children. It was possible that "what is there for me" part was not articulated properly. Climate Change is subtle; the children need science appreciation to understand the impact. All education is mentoring.

New people were getting in to the Hall. Laxmi's wife Sudipa walked in; I greeted her. There were various other people coming in, greeting each other. It feels awkward when people greet each other in semi- private setting when one is not introduced. I felt strange in my place, not a welcome feeling. Laxmi entered the room finally. There were people setting up the PA system. Laxmi introduced me to Dr. Nanda sitting right behind me. I was stunned that I had not noticed him. He was my favourite teacher in college. He taught Chemistry, I loved his delivery. Forty-five years have passed. He got up and greeted me, I felt humbled. I went and sat next to him. We had great association in college. Dr. Nanda had retired as the Chair of Chemistry in the University. He was having bad health; but has recovered. Then next to him was my friend Dr. Naik of Zoology. Dr. Naik was two years' senior in college, but we associated. He did research at Columbia University and then taught in Indian Institute of Science at Bangalore. Now he was associated with the National Institute of Science Education and Research in Bhubaneswar. Next to him was Dr. Das of Chemistry, who was in the faculty during my time. Dr. Kar and Dr. Panda were next to him. They were in Kanpur IIT. They had visited me in Cambridge with Laxmi. Dr. Patnaik of Mathematics sat in front. I felt at home. I had gone back in time. It was delightful!

Laxmi opened the meeting with a brief report on the organization. He said it was a non-hierarchical NGO with focus on energy, education, environment and health. He narrated issues in each of these areas and suggested that the goal would be to find innovative solutions to address issues of cheaper energy, better education, cleaner environment and stronger health. It was a bold grass root effort driven by people in the academy where new technical ideas could be developed and transferred for prototype. The goal was to explore cost-effective solutions. The report was written in English; I would have preferred if done in Oriya.

Dr. Nanda was the first speaker. He always looked sharp, professorial. He said that the education had suffered because the students were questioning less. He shared the view that questioning sharpened understanding and expanded the analysis. His suggestion was that the best teacher solicited questions and addressed them. I agreed. A beautiful movie before could have been a great educational experience for the children had it been followed up with tons of questions. Someone had to encourage and handle the questions. Resources were in short supply.

Dr. Nanda was given a plaque on behalf the organization. Everybody had ten minutes of time. The next was I. I took permission to speak in Oriya. I emphasized that questioning needs rendering a thought, and so there was need of fluency in a language. We are only creative in our own native language and it takes a long time to gain fluency in a foreign language. Then I went on my theory of treating mind as a sensor that creates negative sensing. Our goal in yoga was to neutralize the negative sensing such that our intake was positive. We need be analytic to ask such that we extend an idea than kill it. The teachers need be positive to take all questions diligently.

An Odissi[59] music master from Puri[60], Pandit Mahapatra, presented a lecture on devotion and its role in reducing stress. An entrepreneur engineer from Hyderabad showed the results from a new design of a solar cooker. The target was to give hot meals to schoolchildren. The cooker retained energy for the cloudy days making it different. The effort was commendable; it was affordable by the village community. Then we had a lecture on cure and prevention of genetic diseases by using native traditional application of oils, herbs and powders. Finally, our friend from Prachi valley presented the visuals of the recently discovered icons and sculptures. The plaque protocol followed to all speakers.

After the lecture, it was time for music. The Odissi teacher had a team of musicians with him and the group presented a set of beautifully composed Odissi songs. Odissi is special; it has a story telling aspect to it. The music is composed in an improvisational style that adds liveliness to a performance. The rendering is emotion driven and the music follows the emotion. After a long time, I was enjoying the original art form of Odissi I had witnessed as a child. The structure and the methodology of Odissi music are not well documented. Like Odissi dance, Odissi music is a separate genre among the known schools of music in India. Everybody was given a snack packet. There was a sense of gratitude for a pleasant and informative evening.

We had arranged our rickshaw to return about 9:30 PM and he was waiting dutifully outside. Some of the taxi drivers are loyal and diligent, I felt extremely happy to see

---

[59]*The traditional art form from Odisha (Orissa), signature in painting, dance, music, clothing and food.*
[60]*The centre of Odissi culture, the home of the famous SriJagannatha Temple.*

him. We rode back to my sister's house. Back there, evening seemed to be just starting up. There was commotion, laughter and movement. I met many new visitors and family members. Now the house was a crowded dorm. We had many pleasant conversations. Bed space was rationed; we had to find our own niche to sleep somewhere. I was allotted a spot. I took a little food and slept.

DAY-6

CUTTACK[61] INSTITUTIONS

Pre-Wedding Ritual

It was the penultimate day to the wedding. Everybody was up early. There were some special rituals in the morning. The women had assembled in the living room and were putting together a handicraft that looked interesting. I did not know the significance of the assembled object. It appeared like something that would be set up in a ritual. My sister had a small ante-room that she used as a worship room; she maintained a shrine. The object made out of a clay jar covered with coloured cloth was now set near the shrine. More wedding related objects were assembled. There was a ritualistic prescription of objects for the priests. I did not have much confidence on the modern-day priests; they seemed to be more involved in counting money than understanding the significance of the faith. After I developed some facility in Sanskrit, I did observe more. I held my opinion to myself; these were not

---

[61]*Cuttack is the principal city in Odisha. An old military town known for the filigree work and jewelry making.*

times for discussion. We needed faith; others from outside were coming in to modify the faith.

The bride Mimi was a sweet daughter. She was bright and intelligent; always spoke with a measured tone. She did engineering studies at a local institution and came out top in the class. She chose to work for a while. She was employed with one of the outsourced service companies, presently posted in Calcutta. Through her employment interview process, she met her fiancé. They liked each other. The earlier system of parents getting involved to find a match for their child is gradually becoming obsolete among the educated youth. A woman seeks security in marriage. Mimi was comfortable with her choice. It is said that a man must provide for the woman, but those were the old days. These days both the man and the woman earn; both compete in their professions. I like women's economic independence. It reduces home stress and helps earn respect from the in-laws. Both of my sisters, my wife and my daughter are economically independent. My mother wanted that way!

Everyone sat down around the dining table for a tea break; we had pleasant conversation. Nobody seemed to be in stress. I admired that. After tea, I went out to the balcony to read the morning paper, my old habit to keep track of the world. The news in the local paper was only local; possibly covering an area a hundred mile around. There was high frequency of accidents, fires or fistfights. News on corruption and scandals filled pages. Anybody in power seemed to be doing something scandalous. There was news from Puri on the events relating to the Car Festival where the priests beat up some foreign worshipper. The priests think they own the deity; the foreigners think that their devotion could only sanctify if they touch the deity.

There is conflict between these two thoughts. The newspaper reported the physical fight that ensued. They did not report the progress of a spacecraft or achievements of people in the world. These did not seem to have much news value for the local public. The newspapers are supposed to educate! As a kid, I used to read the newspaper loud to my maternal grandfather. Those were the days of Sputnik and beginning of space missions. These days, science was taking more challenging projects that needed to come to the public knowledge.

I overheard discussion in the other room about some stuff that was supposed to be dispatched on behalf of the bride's mother's family. There is no real theory how we hear signal in noise. After hearing more carefully I went to check. There was a whole list of goods that I was supposed to be responsible on behalf of the mother's parental family. I felt irresponsible. I had not asked, nobody told me either. It was expressed as a social obligation. I could not joke it away. In my sister's house, it was an alien camp. I expressed my inability to assemble the objects and said that I would wait for my other sister to show up. Both of us would try collecting the goods. Apu showed up and I expressed my concern to her. She told me in a cool manner that it had been taken care of and that Gita has arranged it all. While we were discussing, Gita entered with a huge plate in hand. The plate was loaded with various items, small and large; it looked decorative. Gita was knowledgeable about the social needs. She was an asset in these situations. Her plate became the centrepiece. All of them were told to offer further gifts; I added cash in an envelope to the plate. The plate symbolized the collective blessings led by the mother's parental family. The mother's brothers were expected to be the protectors of the bride in her new home!

Visit to Uncle's House

I had planned to go to Cuttack to visit my mother's brothers. She had a sister who died young. My mother's older brother died not completing fifty. Out of her five younger brothers, three had already passed away. The last two lived in a house in Cuttack in a section called Mahatab Road. Out of two of surviving brothers of my mother, the older one was a lawyer. He was a bright man, a precocious student. Being busy with the family affairs, he could never take time out to get married. The younger uncle married late. He was blessed with a daughter. The aunt had been diagnosed with some difficult disease lately. Besides them, Jitu's widow mother lived in the residence. Three other widow aunts lived with their children in the neighbouring towns.

My mother's family was ejected from their ancestral home suddenly; and they took residence in our apartment in town in the early '50s. They took separate residence afterwards and I would spend considerable time in their house. The last two uncles and I would walk together to school; they acted as my escort. My grandfather was affectionate to me. I loved him very much. He was a dignified man. When dressed up, he would look like how an old Oriya might have looked in their prosperous days; tall, handsome, upright; high forehead and strong jaws. I had not examined the circumstances under which they had to leave their village estate. My grandfather tipped me liberally and I would do tasks he would ask for. Mostly the tasks would be to give him a cup of tea or to read newspaper to him. He knew the limitations of an under-teen boy.

My mother leaned on her brothers in times of her need. My father would be away in detention or in public work for long stretches of time; the uncles would be summoned to come and stay with us. They would help us in our homework; assist in chaperoning children and escort mother for her medical check-ups. They helped in grocery and in purchasing clothes and gifts. The youngest brother was of special liking to my mother; I did not know the "baby" in the family concept in those days. Sometimes I would compete with my youngest uncle to gain my mother's attention.

I had more work to do at Cuttack. I had thought of visiting my graduating High School, where my father also graduated. My intention was to negotiate a prize in the school in my father's honour. Then I would go to my graduating college where my father also graduated. I wished to institute a prize for literature and language in the college. Then I would visit my old Cultural club and return. A young friend in the extended family helped arrange a taxi for me and the taxi had arrived. I took a quick shower and started my journey.

The expansion of the road connecting Bhubaneswar to Cuttack was the only visible infrastructure project in Orissa[62] during the last thirty years. It took several years of work. It was operational. One could make the highway trip between the twin cities in fifteen minutes; reaching the high way from the town was a different matter. The earlier one lane road with sharp bends had taken many fatalities; it was a danger trip with massive trucks sharing the road with tiny scooters. Now there was space, and there was air to breathe. The technique of dangerous driving was there but there was room to manoeuver. On both sides, traffic did go in wrong directions for shorter rides. Such

---

[62] *The earlier name for Odisha. The change is slowly creeping in.*

practice is the signature of the old-world freedom; they would cause problems in the future. Habits do die hard!

We passed the Kathjodi river bridge on way to Cuttack. The taxi driver asked me if we could bypass the regular road and go via the river way. I agreed. I wished to see the river close. Cuttack is sandwiched between two major rivers, Mahanadi and Kathjodi. Actually, Mahanadi splits into two about ten miles west from Cuttack; Kathjodi is the branch. Cuttack was a fort and a trade centre in older times. The modern town sits below the river level and is prone to floods during the monsoons. My first exposure to public works was to reach out to people in the flooded areas. Water piled up easily, several feet could run on the roads if the rainfall rate increased to a few inches an hour.

We reached Mahtab Road. It was not easy to find the right lane towards the house. One only remembered landmarks. They change through demolition or extension. Varanasi also has lanes, but the layout is frozen; no new construction happens in the old city. Cuttack was different, construction continued. There was no real planning on traffic, communications or power. Massive migration from the surrounding areas was happening. There was not much incentive in farming these days; everyone was after a service job equipped with a tiny liberal arts education. The British engineered the system to prepare clerks to staff the offices, but now the offices are saturated. The cities had massive unemployment. I had heard that the roads were unsafe in the night. The old cultural Cuttack was buried by the layer of new transient youth looking for something to do; more often they were into crime.

I negotiated the road and spotted the house. Pradeep from Delhi was in Cuttack; he opened the door. I met the aunts and the youngest uncle. The daughter was in school.

The aunt cried expressing distress on her sickness. Severe disease diagnosis was not well done in India. Patients can feel helpless. She was in the last phases of her therapy treatment and was expected to recover. I spoke to all. I gave them the sarees I had brought from Delhi; they expressed thanks. The older uncle was in High Court. Pradeep and I sat down for lunch. I had more in my day ahead.

The older aunt was a good cook. I loved her cooking. The style was very local and was just right to my taste. Cuttack had native vegetables; the local style was to cook with juice from the vegetables. Not many know. It is traditional, needs preservation. She came from a neighbouring village. Her brother studied with me in college. She became a widow at a relatively young age. Her four children are married now; Pradeep is the youngest. Jitu passed away a year after Pradeep's wedding. A daughter lived nearby and was a teacher. Another daughter lived a hundred mile away. They took care of their mother. Aunt herself was very religious, visited temples and listened to discourses several days a week. She joined me in chanting the Gita when my father passed away.

Visit to High School

I asked Pradeep to join me in my trip to my old High School. We quickly went towards the river and followed the river for a few miles. The familiar scenes showed up. I visited these roads every so many years to come to the main branch of the State Bank. A good friend of mine lived on a parallel street, but I always got lost once I entered the housing areas. We spent considerable time in those streets, but the landscape had changed, it was utterly crowded now. The roads were too narrow, encroached with vendor's stalls. In some areas, half the road was used as sewer drain. One felt helpless to observe the age of the roads, there was little maintenance. The river way was good; it had been extended to be a perimeter road. One could get to the highway east or west easily. It was hard to travel inside the town.

We descended from the river way near a block of yellow coloured buildings. These buildings had been there from the early days, they housed various State offices. The Teachers' Training College was behind them. Further down was our school. We had to go through the front-gate that opened towards the High Court. We went through an area that had the red coloured buildings. They always looked old and busy. They had offices of land registry and various litigation courts. Litigation for land was common and various small court lawyers made a business out of it. They prolonged friction and made the conflict deeper. Litigation happened among the family members and that was the sad part of the new-found freedom. Families broke; property liquidated through litigation.

Vendors of different kinds shielded the school-gate. We used to buy food from those vendors during our school days. Some of the food was tasty. The current young people settled for a flat taste. I asked the driver to find a spot to park. There was no designated area. It was chaotic. Like elsewhere more buildings had shown up, there was litter on the road. We carefully opened the gate and entered. There were bicycles everywhere; more students were riding bikes to school, a good sign. I peeped in to the large room right at the gate; the room was earlier used for vocational training. There were no tools inside. The sign said it was a Childcare Centre, but there were no children to be seen. Next to it, there was a small children's park. These were new; times have changed. We reached the Headmaster's office. We let the clerk know of our arrival. We waited.

Ravenshaw Collegiate is the oldest High School in Orissa. It came to operation as an English medium private school called Cuttack School in 1822. Later, it was taken over by the Government. It became a High School called Cuttack Zilla School in 1851. Afterwards, the building hosted intermediate and law classes until these moved to their new spaces. The school took the name of T. E. Ravenshaw in 1875 in honour of the then English Commissioner, who helped during the preceding Orissa famine. Hostel facilities were available for the out of station students. Equipped such, the school remained as the premier educational institution for decades in the State until other schools were established in Cuttack and elsewhere. Later, P. M. Academy, Mission High School, Ranihat High School and Board High School added distinction to Cuttack.

After its centenary in 1954, the school was scheduled to try out the new Higher Secondary curriculum. Mine was the third batch in Higher Secondary to graduate from the school. I entered the grade IX in 1959. The school admitted children of Government officials by default and others on merit. I was a transfer student admitted because of my scholarship grades in the Middle School. I enjoyed my time in the new School. The day was packed with activities; the teachers were excellent, affectionate and friendly. There was enough freedom to think and play. I was involved in science, writing, organizing, drama and competitions. I had made great friends. Sri Nanda Kishore Rath who came in as Headmaster in 1960 was awarded the President's Medal in 1963.

This was my first visit to the School since my

graduation in 1963. We were called in to the Headmaster's office. It was a familiar room. The School prizes were displayed in the back cabinet. A board on the wall had bold print names of students who had done well in the last twenty years. I thought this to be a good addition. There were a few pictures of some of the famous personalities from Orissa on the other wall. The Headmaster cordially invited us and offered us chairs. He looked young in age, certainly less than sixty. In India, the Headmaster is a prized position for a public-school teacher; Ravenshaw Collegiate was blessed to have some of the best teachers as Headmasters.

The present Headmaster, Pradeep and I went out and walked the corridors. The school had IVth grade to Xth Grade, the final two grades of our time did not exist anymore. The Headmaster complained that they had lost the selection criteria in admissions because of a legislative ruling. The admission was not selective any more. The new legislation apparently waived the tests in the lower grades. It was a blunder to an educationist. The Headmaster claimed that the student body was less homogeneous and the school excellence was compromised. While I am against elitism, we need resources to educate children. The teachers need motivation; good motivated students are the catalysts in making a teacher give more to his or her profession. A student is the only possession a teacher has. To draw good people to teaching is also to have good students in school. The education policy creates a new order of market tutorials that have become parallel institutions drowning out the regular ones. Many teachers are involved in such enterprise, reducing their efforts in their regular job.

We entered the big hall next to the Headmaster's office. This was used as a library and as a meeting hall. I had read many plaques presented to the dignitaries, teachers and students in that hall. Presently it had no furniture, the pictures of the old Headmasters were there on the wall; all with a good coat of dust. I asked about the apathy in maintenance. He said there was little provision of maintenance in the school budget. I wanted to clean the pictures, did do some; but did not want to show off my emotion publicly. I began to feel hurt. My school had gone old and there was no caretaker. I had left it; I did not find time to ask. I felt troubled.

We moved on. The children looked smaller, possibly the lower classes were more populated. There is a school uniform these days. We entered a room that is used as a Teachers' common room. I introduced myself, had a chat with some of the teachers, and we moved on. The large room in the corner had converted to be the library. We did not use much of the school library during our days, but the world has changed. The boys and girls must know what is happening round the world, they must know advances in space, engineering, health sciences and computers. They must have enough exposure to compete in the new world. Pure creativity is to be supplemented with information.

I like libraries. Thought came to me that I should help the school to renovate and modernize the library. I walked further. I saw the dangling wires and the broken glass. There were old desks lined up in the middle not in a very inviting manner. There was a full-time librarian and another assistant to help with the computers. I discussed the possible renovation plans with the Librarian and the Headmaster. The Headmaster was particularly interested and said that some thought was given earlier, but funds did not show up. A Managing Committee ran the school, and the Committee considered new plans. I kept that in mind and made an internal determination to pursue the matter. My thought has been that the quality of our people was a function of their appreciation of the world of knowledge when they are young. Since the teacher to student ratio was disproportionately against the teacher, we must create new tools to engage the children. We needed work in mathematics, sciences, writing, literature and philosophy. We needed to enable children to think large. We had to work on this front.

We walked further in the school. There was litter on the ground; the Headmaster said there was only one caretaker who came once a week to clean the three-acre property. I talked about student volunteering, but then I remembered that the children were in a low age range. We came to a new building now dedicated as a Computer Laboratory. There were computers in the room, but they did not appear to be in use. There was a teacher for the lab; the classes were not coordinated for sharing the resource. I felt bad for the dust and low upkeep of the machines. Technology needed care in order to be of use; dust and water are the most unwelcome enemies of electronics. I did not see any solution except to help create a climate-controlled room; but then I thought that we have to find a general solution applicable to India's conditions. We have to wait to learn what people can manage.

I wanted to visit my old Science Club room. The Headmaster said that it was active, but the concerned teacher was absent. There were no extra keys; they looked around, but no luck. We returned to Headmaster's office. The Headmaster had ordered some cold drinks. I wanted to learn about the student performance. The Headmaster gave me a copy of the annual magazine and a copy of the school yearbook. I was glad to see the magazine. We could not revive the magazine during our school years. It was full-fledged publication now with student articles, teacher essays and various graphics. I liked the humour strips. The never-ending retinue of messages from all kinds of people bothered me. Subservience to officialdom is an old colonial ritual. We must destroy it for any progress.

Saroj, the High School friend

It was time to move to my next appointment. I called the Vice Chancellor of Raveshaw University[63], Dr. Tripathy. Ravenshaw was the college I graduated from, also my father did. Dr. Tripathy advised to see him at 5 PM in his home. He was leaving college; I got a bit disappointed. I called my school friend Saroj to check if he would join. Saroj agreed and I proceeded to his house that was nearby. These are old areas of Cuttack; the roads were done for the horse-carts. The narrow roads were presently used for two-way traffic causing enormous problem. Added to this was the parking of motorbikes that could cover a significant fraction of the road. People parked next to the place of business or residence; there were no designated parking areas. There was general accommodation when a traffic problem showed up, but nobody tried to avoid the problem. Bike thieves existed and they operated with ingenuity. Security was a personal problem. One could not think about it. It was a larger issue.

Saroj was delighted to see me. We had spent many afternoons and evenings in that house doing homework. We used the inner courtyard for drama practice. In the

---

[63]*The former Ravenshaw College has lately been updated to be an autonomous university.*

earlier days, we operated as family members in each other's house and Saroj's house was special. His mother was extra gracious and we would have our meals there on many occasions. Affection filled old memories flashed by and challenged me if I was up to the mark wherever I lived. Hospitality is a function of time and resources, but above all, it is of heart. We certainly try, but we cannot match the authenticity of heart in the old world. To make another person feel at home is a signature of air, water and the soil. Warmth is an artifact; the soil has to bless. It possibly happens in historical time scale. We are too individualized abroad.

We talked about our school friends. Two of our classmates had passed away. I inquired about their families. It was not easy for me to meet the bereaved families. Before we remembered them, people leave earth. Our younger friend Narayan showed up. I had recruited him to our Club in 1963. He has developed himself to be a popular director and playwright. I had spoken to him on phone from the US regarding the staging of the Danabira Harischandra *suanga*[64]. When a play is performed mostly in songs it is called a *suanga*, it is an abridged version of the original play. Our Club turns fifty in 2013 and we wanted to give the process a start. Narayan showed me his edited script and we sang a few songs together. I was happy that he was moving forward even though the time was short. The production date would be July 6.

Saroj's wife was sick. She had been having medical problems for some time. Occasionally she would not be

---

[64] *An old presentation art form where a story is presented through dramatic lyrics.*

able recognize people. I was one of the few she recognized. I had seen her when she first came as a bride. Her face looked as fresh as she was forty years ago. She took my hand and put on her head, a version of a reverse greeting. One of her hands was not mobile. I admired her dignity and her poise. She had a daughter and a son in the US. She was a good mother to them and always thought about them. Saroj was exemplary in providing care for his wife; Jyotsna indeed was as beautiful and as delicate as her name would indicate.

Visit to the Vice Chancellor

I proceeded towards the vice chancellor's house accompanied by Saroj and Pradeep. We passed by Victoria School, an inner-city school established by the famous nineteenth century educationist, late Sri Madhusudan Rao. His ancestors came from the Marathas; he spoke Marathi at home. He took interest in Oriya language and composed beautiful prayers and nature poems in Oriya. He created the first Oriya alphabet reader for children in Oriya. His family culture in education owed itself to the *Brâhma*[65] movement; a group that wanted to reform the Hindu faith by getting rid of the rituals. The group starting from Bengal had influenced the intelligentsia in Orissa. *Brâhma* movement was progressive and encouraged education for both men and women.

We passed by the birthplace of Sri Subhas Chandra Bose, popularly known as Netaji in India. He had his childhood in Cuttack and did graduate from Ravenshaw Collegiate before moving to Calcutta. The birthplace was

---

[65] *A reform movement in nineteenth century initiated in Bengal in an effort to modernize the Hindu beliefs.*

converted to a Museum a few years ago. We did not have time to visit; we moved on. The road was narrow, difficult for a two-way traffic. We came to a wider area and Saroj pointed to me the famous *Chandi*[66] temple. The *Chandi* is the resident deity in the town. My mother visited the Temple every week and appeared to talk to the deity. Many thought, that the deity was alive. They communicated openly like talking to one's mother. Some people visit the Temple daily.

We passed by the Barabati Stadium, a landmark in Cuttack. It opened in 1957. I remembered to have witnessed the National Games of India hosted there in 1958. It was fun to watch the professional athletes do sports and games. To our young eyes, wrestling was the most interesting sport and we would take sides for no obvious reason. We would make our quiz on a wrestler's diet. Young age is romantic. Lately I see people make a living through sports betting, it is a full-fledged business. Then some players join the betting business by adding pretention to the game. Money does indeed corrupt individuals!

We reached the area at Cuttack that had the barracks for the soldiers during the war. After the soldiers left, the barracks housed the administrative offices of the State until buildings were constructed in Bhubaneswar. Bhubaneswar in those days was a small town known as a tourist attraction for its temples. We proceeded further; the area was called the Cantonment, where military officers had their quarters. These spacious residences were considered prized houses in the modern times. I was happy that the Government had allotted a good accommodation for an educationist.

There was a guard at the gate. He opened the gate

---

[66] *A form of Devî, expressing the whimsical nature.*

for us. We met the Vice Chancellor in the small office in his house. He was a Botanist. He was for a long time at Delhi and is not so familiar with Orissa. Occasionally thought has come if I would be of any use in university administration in Orissa. University is not a big place, but it is multi-disciplinary. It caters to many interests. In the west, they call the head of the University a President. The Harvard President carries a big influence in the governance of the country. Ravenshaw University was no less for Orissa. Anybody from Orissa who had contributed to society had a link to this august institution. The teachers prided themselves for their tenure at the former Ravenshaw College.

The Vice Chancellor talked about the academic reform and the curriculum revision. Apparently, the curriculum has not changed in decades and the question papers were readily available in the market. There had not been much creativity in framing tests to create curiosity among the students. Students wish to enter the work force by showing the diploma than being tested and grilled in their knowledge. Language instruction was particularly poor, since it was made into a routine process. The laboratories needed new equipment, but the funding was not enough for the infrastructure. He said that he was convening a Conference in campus to review the curriculum and invited me to attend. My views on curriculum were based on stressing the fundamental and I thought I might not be a good partner in the local process. It was no point lecturing on change, but we must create the change by participation. The latter was not easy, but I had a wish.

I spoke to him about instituting an Award on my father's name. He was not very familiar with the movements in Orissa, or the Oriya literature. He did not express much enthusiasm. He said many of the current scholarships were not awarded because of insufficient competition. It was indeed a problem. I had noticed the interest and enthusiasm among the new youth was less towards literature, elocution, drama or composition. Some people played sports but nothing of high skill category. In order to find candidates in Oriya literature, we have to first create infrastructure work in the library and sponsor many study clubs and class seminars. This needed willing teachers to mentor and assist. We were candid in our assessment. I had to say that I would do my bit to promote the literature studies along with other professional studies. The idea of scholarship was temporarily shelved

Carnival[67] at Kathjodi

We had tea with him and were ready to leave. I had to drop Saroj back and then go to the riverbanks where a summer carnival (jâtrâ) was being organized. The carnival attracted people from the neighbouring villages. Trade guilds for exchange of goods would show up. It is a nice place to purchase of household items. The carnival in November is famous. Called Bali Jâtrâ it is a remnant of the market gathering before the sailors departed on their voyage to Bali in Indonesia. Bali has a large population following Indian culture. The sailors from Orissa created the settlements. The brides from Bali were prized. In those days in early Christian era Orissa was prosperous. The current carnival was not so big. A new group organized it

---

[67] *A folk gathering of ancient origin held on religious observances. Could be a legacy of the old harvest festival.*

to take advantage of the end of summer weather to create a social forum.

There were various neon lights and decorations. The place was crowded. The driver dropped us off and went away to park at a distance. We would communicate via the cell phone. Everybody spoke on the cell phone; it has been a great medium for people to coordinate. We waded our way through the crowd to reach an auditorium area. There was a dance program going on. Odissi dance was popular and was a normal addition to a cultural event. I was there to witness a scheduled performance of our club Sanskruti Vihar. They were supposed to take stage after the dance item. I had to be careful with my schedule. Late night travel was risky.

The dance program ended. Various individuals showed up on stage and extolled how good the event had been. They started congratulating each other; I thought it was excessive. Then a person came and said how grateful he was for the presence of a holy man who would speak next. Since I like philosophical discourses, I wanted to check it out. After a few other persons expressed their obeisance, the holy man took stage wrapped in saffron robes. He started saying some elementary things in a tired voice. It was disappointing. There was a whole league of such holy men who exhibit their vanity around the towns. They made a living by making tired speeches on do's and don'ts. Some of the articulate ones did show up abroad. They collect money for their subsistence or for some supposedly philanthropic work. The modern practice of Hindu religion needed a huge clean up!

The speech continued and it was of no value. I could gauge from the noise level that others were equally disinterested; nobody stopped him. Had I been a local resident I would object to such operation, but I did not wish to stick out. Pradeep and I got up and we proceeded towards the back stage to check my old friends from the club. There they were; it was a beautiful reunion. I met about half a dozen of our members. They would be performing a musical piece on a famous Islamic devotee of Jagannatha, who wrote immortal songs. Salabega was a poet born of a Hindu woman and an Islamic soldier during the time of Muslim invasion of Orissa in the seventeenth century. He is acknowledged as the prime devotee of Jagannatha for emotion in his words expressing devotion.

    I begged leave of my friends. Pradeep coordinated traffic for the car to show up. We returned. I dropped Pradeep at his residence and travelled back to Bhubaneswar. I reached Bhubaneswar at about 9 PM.

DAY-7

WEDDING EVENT

Wedding Preparation

Caste is a tight social concept in India. The word is Portuguese, but the social classification of people in India goes back to the Vedas. Originally, the classification was called *varGa*[68] in Sanskrit, the meaning could be one that describes an object. This definition was based on a person's aptitude and hence a category could be defined that characterized the person's aptitude. Four varGas were recorded; people who liked to study were called *BrâhmaGa*[69] (Brahmin in modern English), people who liked martial arts were called *Kcatriya*, people who liked farming were called *Vaiœya*, and people who liked to help but otherwise remained leisurely were called *S'ûdra*. It was a product of a conceptual division of an anthropomorphic divinity, with the head, trunk, hands and legs purporting to do different functions for the body.

---

[68] *A social classification initiated during the Vedic period to distinguish people with aptitudes.*
[69] *Written through a transliteration scheme for proper pronunciation. Please refer to https://en.wikipedia.org/wiki/Devanagari_transliteration*

Each is necessary, but each is different; together they made the whole.

India's social history has been a competition between these classes, one trying to establish superiority against the other. *BrâhmaGa*s have been the scholars, the *Kcatriya*s were the rulers, *Vaiœya*s were the businesspersons and the *S'ûdra*s were the farmers. In course of time each of these groups showed hundreds of variations depending on what books they read, or what military craft they knew, the type of trade they did, or the kind of work they offered. Each of the activities made a guild for themselves and made it a family profession than that of personal aptitude. This became the modern practice of caste, which created a designation by birth and not by skills. It is a degradation of the original concept. All groups hold their cards tight since the privileges were set up by the rulers. Through the theories of reincarnation and various other interpretations of karma, one group can claim that its profession was superior to the others giving it a higher social security. All such theories have no scientific value.

In Orissa, two of these birth classes compete. One is *BrâhmaGa*; the other is *KaraGa*, a subset of *Kcatriya*. These latter ones were writers of documents, religious and secular. The *BrâhmaGa*s were supposed to be well versed to keep everything in memory. The task of writing was relegated to people who could celebrate the skills in engineering the scripts. High-end calligraphy, sketches in manuscript and ornamentation in page production are the products of this class of people. Because of these skills, they became very valuable in society and carried high prestige. Though *BrâhmaGa*s kept the upper hand as priests, the *KaraGa*s developed themselves to be a close second. In the present day, Orissa, the skills of of these groups have disappeared, but the vanity of belonging one group or the other manifests in social setting.

The wedding rituals of these two groups are different. The principal difference is timing. The *BrâhmaGa*s hold them during the daylight hours; the *KaraGa*s celebrate in the coolness of the night. The wedding of my niece is scheduled for the unearthly hour of 3AM. While it sounds odd to me, the rest in the household is quite comfortable with it. In a *BrâhmaGa* wedding, the guests are fed after the wedding, but here the feast is beforehand. The sociology of the two groups is different. I have not been inside a *KaraGa* wedding earlier. My sister's husband comes from an established *KaraGa* family; things would be done as prescribed by a family priest who happens to be a *BrâhmaGa*. *BrâhmaGa*s made the books and created the set up for others to follow; let the night shift belong to someone else!

Because of my ignorance on the intricacies of the rituals, I had been excused from any service role except just to show up. That gave me an opportunity to observe things. Apu's husband Basanta would be officiating on behalf of us. The tall handsome man loved the rituals. The principal skill is to sit in a confined space for several hours and listen to some incorrectly pronounced Sanskrit phrases. One had to accept the situation and show happiness and gratitude to the priests. Any irritation could affect the future of the new couple. One had to be patient. Basanta and Apu showed up, they talked like seasoned hands. Various rights and wrongs were discussed. A consensus was achieved.

An important person in all this is the family barber, who is imported from the hometown. Indian barbers are smart and shrewd. I have not explored how they use their skills in a wedding. The barbers are also known for their great massaging skills. The new barber noticed my fatigue and suggested that I take a massage. I wilfully agreed and we both disappeared to a roof top room. Before he applied his techniques on me, somebody yelled from below and he had to return. Attempt to make money from two jobs for the same hours could be the signature of shrewdness. My body ache remained. After days of travel and movement, I was a bit down. There were symptoms of dehydration, a typical outcome in travel.

There was discussion about the hospitality towards the groom's party. Many had arrived. They were booked in a few of the local hotels. More were expected before the evening. We had to have the accommodation ready. Unlike the western situation, the number in the party is a flexible count; the bride's party should be ready for any eventuality. In the new social order, it could be a test of bride's family's wealth and prestige. Because of the wedding season, all hotels were booked. Anjan, Lakhi and I took a trip to look at some of the recently finished apartments that could be used for the night. Anjan and Lakhi owned them; but had neglected to fix the plumbing and electricity. The mattresses and furniture needed to be rented; there was plumbing and running water in the unit. The view from the balcony was towards the town and one could see twenty miles or more. There were beautiful spaces for garden with abundant sunshine, but nobody seemed to be interested.

A wedding planning has various management decisions. Professional wedding planners could be available in big cities. In places like Bhubaneswar, the decisions are ad hoc and are managed by the family and their friends. The wedding would take place in a market like building which had a large hall and had parking facilities. We passed by the facility. I learned that it was one of the good locations in town. Others offered their services. The very rich people and people who needed to show stronger social status hosted these in some artificial Vegas type settings. I had only heard of this extravaganza from people and imagined their opulence. Apparently, politicians who happened to be in the Government for some time owned some of these facilities. It was possible that some of the road construction money showed up in these facilities after changing a few hands. In my sister's case, they were trying their best to celebrate their daughter within the means at their disposal. To host an Indian wedding is an expensive operation.

We reached back home. The bride was now getting ready for the wedding. Hands, body and face were being decorated with various plant dyes and flower juices to get the bridal look. The juice from the henna plant is popular; there could be other dyes. Since these happen rarely, many of the bride's unmarried friends also make themselves tattooed as a rehearsal to their future weddings. Freestyle hand painting on palm or hand needs skills. There are special women who practice these skills. Each family has one in their rolls and many others show up to offer their expertise. The painting needs to match with the jewellery that the bride would use along with the colour of the new dress. The preparation could take several hours. A few of Mimi's co-workers from Calcutta had shown up along with some classmates from her college days. They seemed to be a happy bunch of young professionals, chattering all the time. They occasionally argued freely about film and music personalities in India and the US.

I had lunch with the family, and then met Rabi Dash who arrived with the proof of the new book of my father. It is a four-hundred-page book. Dr. Debi Prasanna Patnaik, the renowned linguist of India, wrote the introduction.

After serving as the Director of Central institute Indian Languages in Mysore for many years, he retired and resides presently in Bhubaneswar. He was my mentor when I arrived in Poona as an Air India Fellow in 1969. Almost every day, he would drive me to his house in Deccan College campus; and we would talk about Orissa, India and languages. For a young man uprooted from home, his courtesy was a godsend. I read his introduction and admired the technicality and respectfulness in it. Rabi Dash had made efforts to create a good cover design; I appreciated.

Wedding Reception

It was time to think on the wedding reception. The dress to wear to an Indian wedding reception is an interesting puzzle to me. In the US and abroad, men put on western style suits and women show up in their elegant silk saris. The asymmetry did appear like clowning to me, but no one talked about it. I had felt that it was unnecessary for men to imitate the western style; and could resort to an Indian alternative as their spouses do. Most Indians did not possess any Indian alternative as formal wear. Rental companies did not rent out Indian dresses as they did with the tuxedos. I had tried to put on a dhoti and a kurta on occasion, but people thought I was not respectful to the parties involved. In India, it had to be different, since people did have access to Indian dresses. Lately some Delhi entrepreneurs were flooding the market with long kurta having opulent embroidery. Many young people were getting used to these and they moved around as mini *Jehangir*[70]s without the necessary

---

[70] *A Moghul prince of luxurious habits.*

moustache or the looks of ferocity. These were also getting popular among the adults. In north India, such dresses were becoming the tradition. In the south, they put on *lungi*[71]*s* or *dhoti*[72]*s*, and a shawl or shirt to cover the chest. In Orissa, the popular dress is *dhoti* and I am carrying mine from the US. I bought a white *kurta*[73] from Delhi that I would use.

    I dozed off a bit on the sofa in the balcony. Dozing led to full sleep. By the time, I was up, everyone was gone. A family cousin told me that my ride was arranged with my sister at 7 PM. I took a wash and got ready with my all white formal dress. I wanted to look like a family elder. These were new roles to assume; the presentation was important. Apu and Basanta arrived and we were on our way to the wedding venue. The car dropped us off at a side entrance. It disappeared to park somewhere. There were not many people at that entrance. It had some casual decoration. I wanted to stick around outside to receive guests, but I was told that almost everyone had arrived and I should go inside. I walked in.

    It was a hall of about 60 feet by 40 feet with a stage erected on the further side. There were twenty or so circular tables with chairs around and several rows of chairs in the back. I met my cousin Dr. Seba, who had retired as the Director of Health in the Government. We were friends from our high school days and loved our association. She was the oldest daughter of my father's younger sister, Bishnupriya. Many other people were moving around and

---

[71] *A cotton dress wrapped around the waist, popular in the southern India.*
[72] *Cotton lower body dress used by men in the northern India.*
[73] *A stitched top dress made popular after the Islamic rule in India.*

I did not know them. The novelist Bibhuti Patnaik showed up. His wife is an older sister to Anjan and they had special links to the wedding. He admired my father deeply and congratulated me on the efforts to republish the book. Meanwhile a whole block of my cousins showed up. They were all married and had children. We were now a group of thirty strong in our contingent. Then my father's youngest brother showed up from Puri with his children and their families. I was relieved that we had a leader who was local and would know the rules better than I did.

Meanwhile the food was being set on the line of tables set along the walls. On one side, there was a snack bar; the drinks were next. No alcohol was served. There was a tendency to show off opulence in wedding receptions, possibly to create an impression among the visiting party. The *Devîmâhâtmya*[74] says that one of the endowed qualities of human beings is to get fooled, and we are fooled easily. Things that glitter, attract us. The protocol in this hall was that individuals would go and get their food and eat wherever they can. Unrestricted consumption was the hallmark of a good old country reception. In our teenage years, we would visit several such receptions per evening. The hosts loved if we showed up. Indian hospitality centred around food!

Young men dressed in crimson jackets and blue ties were operating each serving table. The dress did not suit most of them. I wondered if some marketing was involved. Nobody else was putting on a jacket; it was the middle of summer in India. The tables had gone messy with spilled food; the architecture of serving food in modern India in some fanciful way needed some rethinking. New tables

---

[74] *The book extolling the paly of Devi, also known as Saptaûati*

were set up with ice cream and sweets. Everything was plentiful. Weddings are known for the food they serve, and they prepare much more than what people can eat. In our villages in Puri, there were special traditional dishes made only on auspicious occasions. Special cooks were recruited to accomplish the task. Here in Bhubaneswar, the food was not ritualistic; it was rich and immense. I was reminded of my food restrictions and the ongoing symptoms of dehydration.

Everybody was busy eating, some on the tables, some holding plates sitting on chairs; and some just plain standing. It was chaotic. I had thought of inviting the Odissi singer that I had met a few days back but my sister did not support the idea. I could understand why classical music was not a recipe for such a gathering. Some people were in a mood of sampling food since they would be on their way to other receptions. To show up in wedding receptions and take food there was a social obligation. This could lead to an eventual superficial relationship and false vanity, but I had not studied. In our younger years, we simply chased food.

While I walked up to get some water, I noticed the rows of chairs were occupied by a new set of people. I determined they must be the part of the out of station groom's party. They looked tired. They were stretching themselves on the chairs. They appeared to be Hindi speakers. I was not in my best shape to start a conversation in Hindi. None of them looked at me with any interest. I did not try out myself. They needed rest. Inter-regional marriage relationships were coming up in India. The children spoke English and had no barrier. The adults were stuck with different languages. Language brings culture. The problem is rampant abroad.

Some of the family members went on stage to take pictures with the bride and groom who were seated on the stage. The whole protocol was upside down since there was no wedding yet. I continued to struggle to appreciate the process. In principle, the wedding might not complete itself because of a thousand causes. On the other hand, if the wedding ritual was unimportant, why do we wait until 3 AM? I tried to resolve the issue in my mind and wait. I kept watching people.

Wedding Ritual
While I had gone out for a walk around, the hall went empty. I was guided to a partitioned room where the family members had assembled. There was a decorated platform, six feet by five feet, the priest was sitting facing away from people and Basantababu[75] was seated to his left facing a perpendicular direction. In Indian culture, facing the proper direction is important. Various directions are designated for various individuals. The priest should face the east and the principal in the ceremony should face north. East is auspicious; the rising sun the welcome omen. North is also good; heat and rains come to India when sun travels north. Heat and rains are welcome signs. The idea was that there were natural powers that guarded the directions and one must appease them for a successful journey in life. Embedded in the culture from ancient times, people were sensitive to it; nobody wanted to break it knowingly. Stories warned horrendous mishaps when anyone ever broke the protocol. The protocol has been followed since the Vedic times!

---

[75] *Babu as a suffix is occasionally added to show respect. The term came from the neighburing Bengal.*

There was a second priest seated to the right of the head priest facing south. He belonged to the visiting party and was to assist the head priest in the ceremony. They chanted many of the Sanskrit stanzas together; I noticed that they mostly repeated their chants. Chants are important. Through the chants, the natural forces were invoked. Natural iconic forces would arrive and be witness to the wedding; bless the couple. Priests did not explain the significance. People assumed them a part of the wedding ritual. More chants continued. Small structures were made using rice grains, vegetable powders and flowers. Metal pots filled with water sat on the structures. They were sanctified with mango leaves.

We were two sections seated on chairs facing the platform. On the left side was the groom's party, about thirty people. The party consisted of mostly men, three or four women. The groom's maternal uncle led the party. The groom's father has passed away and his mother was helping to prepare the ritual in their village when the party would return with the bride. On our side, there were almost all women, very few men. The village-barber friend moved around passing objects in different directions. All people shouted to him to get the object they needed; it could be cloth, wood, oil, water, strings and other ancillary things. The bride was escorted to the stage. She was dressed in a red dress; she looked shy and somewhat uncomfortable with the glare of light. The glare was needed for photography. A video person was recording everything from different views. It would be a memento for the occasion.

Chants were getting soft; I could not hear them. I did not know the procedure, but I followed Sanskrit. It would have been good to be able to hear it all, but I had not positioned myself properly. I only made out a few words. The ritual is a process to simulate commitment; it is an opportunity to visualize the future and create determination. A life always moves with help; we seek out help. The ritual possibly teaches that we could have people and nature around to help us. I did not personally go through a similar procedure. I had no time or opportunity. My family was different; a wedding organization was not a priority. The bride and Basanta are now escorted out and the groom took the seat that faced north. Ritual chanting was done and the groom was given water and flowers to offer on the makeshift shrine.

It was 1 AM. We had to take a two-hour break to wait for the auspicious moment at 3 AM for the second part of the ritual. People were advised to go back to their hotel rooms and return later. There was discussion if the priests could continue without waiting. I belonged in this camp. I voiced my opinion. They concurred and resumed with a ten-minute bathroom break. Suddenly, a young lady in our side got into a bout of uncontrolled laughter. She captured herself back and again laughed with loud noise. I thought it was disrespectful to the gathering, but I could not help. I tried to walk away to exhibit my displeasure; it had no effect on the person. The hysterical laughter continued. I figured out that the person was intoxicated; it was a different late night scene. This was my first experience with unseemly experience with women in an Oriya social gathering. Society does not wait for what I might like or dislike. The new women have possibly a right to be free and liberated; the social norms could be changing.

The next phase of the ritual had to do with fire, called

a *homa*[76]. A *homa* is a Vedic ritual and has two purposes. The first is that the couple commits to each other with fire as the witness. Fire is considered the first among the auspicious ones since it is invoked. It has a whim. The success of creating a controlled fire is a technical achievement for the early man. In a religious way, the fire is used as a sacrificial pit where the couple can drop objects to learn the triumph of life versus the attachment to objects. The couple lives for each other than the objects they procure; it is a subtle lesson. It is a process to teach that one gives away what one has; such giving away can earn virtue in life to oneself and the family. The *homa* is done with various objects offered; these days they have specific *homa* objects that help to sustain the fire. I was not sure if the priests explained to the bride and groom on the sanctity of the ritual.

The maternal uncle in the groom's side and I were seated on both sides of the aisle observing the proceeding. I had tried a few times to gain his attention, but he would not share a glance. Suddenly there was commotion on the other side and he looked agitated. He rushes to the platform. It had something to do with some object to be given to the groom from the bride's side. Anjan, Lakhi and Apu gathered near the platform to diffuse the situation. I was curious, but felt like not to nose around. The matter seemed resolved and the ritual resumed. Now there was commotion in the bride's camp on some similar matters, but the groom's group put down the fire by opening a suitcase and a jewellery box. I thought that the drama was good, but then I thought we need accountability than the

---

[76] *A fire ritual where sacrificial objects are offered in a fire pit. It is a Vedic ritual to alleviate suffering and ward off unforeseen dangers.*

ad hoc show and tell. Everything seemed to be verbal and trust was assumed. The trust was questioned to raise commotion.

The fire ritual ended with the bride and groom going around the fire pit seven times. Ritual vows like the Christian vows, but more elaborate, were uttered by the bride and the groom. After the circumambulation ritual was completed, the priests announced them as husband and wife. Everyone gathered went closer and blessed them with rice and flowers. Rice blessing signifies food and wealth, the flower blessing signifies luck and opportunity. We need both to operate life.

I lingered to talk to some people in the groom's party, but they seemed tired and did not appear inviting. It was late in the night. They needed rest to take the train back next day. I did not pursue further and returned home with Apu.

DAY-8

WEDDING AND FAMILY

Post-Wedding Morning Ritual

I had been observing that language was a general cultural barrier. The bride was not fluent with the Oriya culture and the riddles; she had no choice than to accept some ritualistic protocol without understanding. The groom and their party spoke Hindi and we did not know their riddles and humour. The groom possibly did not care. English is used as a common language of communication, but no one knows how to display the marital riddles, which are a part of the popular literature. I was finding the process dry and mechanical. The melody of an event is in the language of expression and it was missing. We should probably conduct such events in a language understood by the principals, either English or Hindi. The blessings of a Sanskrit mantra would not mean much if they were not understood. I imagined that we were entering a mechanical world than the social world of kinship and togetherness. I felt the absence of my father who used to enliven such situations through plain simple humour.

The groom had spent the night at the house and the women had arranged a ritualistic welcoming event. Multi-coloured flower icons were drawn on a piece of paper with the message of "Happy Wedding" in Oriya and the names of bride and groom were written there. The paper was posted on a blank wall and the couple would sit there to be in a welcoming ritual. This ritual was new to me. The style was possibly imported from the town of Baripada. The couple was given gifts and was blessed by all with rice and flowers. I asked all to join with me in singing the Oriya composition to Sri Jagannatha written by the devotee Salabega, a popular all-purpose prayer. Everybody joined with enthusiasm; there was sonority in the house.

Everybody was served breakfast. There was general relief and mutual patting on the job well done. I admired the large contingent of people who had shown up to assist the bride's family. There was no tension, everyone worked with discipline and patience. Anjan looked relaxed; he does not get tense easily! Their younger daughter Rini was the accountant and the manager of funds. They had minor discussion on various payments. Anjan told me that Rini was tough. She was meticulous in accounting. One needed a tough hand in such undertaking. My sister Lakhi handled the kitchen with the other ladies. Lakhi also did not show exertion. She had help of a dozen women with seasoned experience. She has learned how to listen to people; she gets along well.

Bhagavadgita reading at Uncle's House

I had to depart for Cuttack to my uncle's house. Pradeep has helped to arrange a family union of my mother's family at their house. Following the tradition, we would engage ourselves in a ritualistic reading of

TheBhagavadgita. I got ready and changed my dress. The taxi showed up and I begged leave of the wedding parties. In principle, some could join us if they wanted, but it was not always convenient to carry extra people. Three hours of the *Gita* reading might not be to everybody's taste. I left alone.

Bhubaneswar was spread out and it was a while before one got on the highway. The roads had become congested and it took us about half hour to get out. The highway ran fine and we were in Cuttack in fifteen minutes, another ten minutes to reach the house. My older uncle was home. It was for him we wished to offer the service. The *Gita* reading was done to prepare people for old age and to console them to forget the vagaries of life. The *Gita* preaches action and it has penetrating language to awaken the conscience. My uncle had passed the age where all his older brothers and sisters had passed away, with my mother having been the only one who lived longer. At seventy-two, he was considered old. For reasons not known to others, he was getting bitter and getting irritated easily. The *Gita* reading is a therapy to people who would understand the message. He seemed to be in great mood this morning and I was very happy to observe his younger personality.

The *Gita* is a part of the epic Mahabharata and is considered a religious book, the message is preached by Sri Krishna. The dates for Sri Krishna are not well established; and it appears a fact that the oral message enunciated by Sri Krishna was scripted to a book later. Sri Krishna talks about a Creator and a universal order of 'dharma' that sustains the universe. The Creator might not actively watch every part of the action in the universe, but reincarnates periodically to restore order when the latter gets into heavy disarray. The actions and the restoration are a part of the cosmic design. The Hindus give the Lord Protector a name Vishnu and the followers of the faith believe Sri Krishna to be an incarnation of Vishnu. The followers are called *vaishnava(s)*. A *vaishnava* ritual is prescribed to have a shrine with a SriKrishna image at the place of worship. A makeshift shrine is constructed where a ritual is performed.

Pradeep's mother was deeply religious and knew the ritual well. The shrine consisted of making designs with rice flour on the floor to simulate an auspicious space. An elevation was created with rice and a SriKrishna image was placed on the elevated surface. Every family had its own traditional deity and here they had the child Sri Krishna in a crawling pose. The child SriKrishna has a sweet countenance and *Vaishnava* devotees are known to go ecstatic when they see such an image. I was called upon to perform the daily bath ritual of the deities when the uncles' family would have a death of a near relative. I had seen this image before. The *Vaishnava* faith in Orissa was about a thousand-year-old and was imported by Sri Ramanuja[77] from the south. Sri Chaitanya[78] in the fifteenth century reinforced it. Some followers of Sri Chaitanya are now a part of the worldwide ISKON movement, which appears heavily dogmatized. Like Christianity, they follow the ritual of proselytizing, which is not a Hindu custom.

My uncle was taking great interest in the happenings and that made me happy. We were doing the event to let him know that we cared for him. I admired him deeply.

---

[77] *An eleventh century religious preacher who flourished in south India.*
[78] *The originator of Krishna movement through singing and chanting.*

He was bright, scholarly, upfront and affectionate. He was a mentor to me throughout my schooling and was a friend whenever I needed help. He is an uncle to all my local friends in Cuttack. I was trying to understand the neurological problems in aging. I had spent some time in brain research and the functioning of the brain was interesting to me. Dementia and lack of attention are common problems. My father had. It is not easy on the caregivers. We just want the person to smile back, talk nicely and be in his or her original nature. In the west, they try to treat with some medication; I am not sure of their efficacy. I had experimented with meditation, but that needed coaching and practice. I had a belief that the friendship and family are the best therapy.

    I had invited Dr. Bishnu, the eminent cardiologist in Cuttack to join us in the reading. Dr. Bishnu was a classmate of my uncle in college and had a respectful friendship with him. He was also a strong proponent of rituals and had done work in restoring manuscripts and creating tutorials for people to observe rituals with rigor. I was not so convinced about the ritual aspect of the service, but I admired the Sanskrit language and its diction. I think it is perfect in its expressive capacity and precise in its message delivery. I am a fan of the language having been involved with its promotion and use in the west particularly among the immigrants from India.

    My uncle said that he had invited a priest who was expected to show up. Priests have a tendency to book several clients for the same time slot. They fail to estimate the travel time. Members in the family and the general population believe that priests could make good things happen and give them enormous respect. The priest arrived. We felt happy. He invoked the deity and established the shrine. He set up a small fire pit to use at the conclusion. He prepared my uncle to be the performer in the event, a task he wilfully assumed. A performer takes a vow to be with the ritual until it completes.

The priest began the service by chanting one hundred and eight names of Vishnu. Our friend Dr. Bishnu corrected him in his pronunciation and the priest was not very happy. Dr. Bishnu insisted that proper pronunciation was necessary in a ritual. The tired priest succumbed; his Sanskrit knowledge was insufficient. We started reading the *Gita* text. The doctor's Gita was in Oriya script. In Oriya, we pronounce "ya" as "Ja" if it happened to be in the beginning of a word. "ya" is a semivowel, but becomes a consonant at the beginning of the word. The idea is Vedic in origin; the classical Sanskrit pronunciation eliminates the difference. Another exception is "la" inside a word; it becomes "La" in Oriya. The new phonetics is a bit odd when we read classical Sanskrit like the *Gita*, but we manage. I read in my style, the doctor proceeded in his. Aunt and her granddaughter were also in the reading. My uncle joined in and we were a team. Occasionally the doctor would stop and would guide the rest of us in the procedures.

The *Gita* is splendid poetry. Each word is carefully edited; each word is measured. It would look as though it has been heavily edited to create the rhythm; the message is clean and clear. It analyses the practice of life from the basics. It empowers the reader to help cultivate one's own potential. Pondering and looking back is not for a man of courage, action is. Be determined and follow your line of duty. The results are not in your hands, so why bother. If you move without selfishness, you must win; whatever results out of your unselfish action is the dharma. Do not regret the outcome; just give your best. The message is not dogmatic or sectarian; it is straightforward and secular. There is nobody to evaluate you, you are your evaluator; all knowledge is inside you and you can access it by controlling your mind. Unknown to you, you have infinite potential; just explore and win the world!

I love *Gita*'s poetics and the melody. The words are musical; the meter is easy. I have identified with it ever since I first read it more than forty years ago. Now I read it fluently, I understand the original; I love it more. My happiness is expressed in my rendering. Others notice; they also get inspired. Reading the Gita is a pleasure to me; it speaks our inner voice. We went for about an hour and the priest wanted to leave saying that he would return. We continued for two more hours and concluded the book. I was happy; my uncle was impressed with my work on Sanskrit literature. My grandfather's family members were Sanskrit scholars and studying Sanskrit was encouraged. The reading becomes an offering to my grandfather by default; this made my uncle happy. The younger uncle was also relishing the poetics and we had become a happy family.

It was 4:30 PM; there was no trace of the priest. I suggested that we eat our lunch. Pradeep had arranged specially cooked *Mahaprasada* from the local temple. The Temple cooked food is tasty and is easy on the stomach. I like the recipe and the preparation. My younger brother Abhi showed up. He joined with the rest of us in sitting down in a long line to take our food. My uncles waited for the priest to complete the service. I had to return to Bhubaneswar. The doctor has patients to be seen in his clinic. We got up, washed our hands and begged leave of all. Abhi joined me in my return trip. We dropped Dr. Bishnu in his clinic and got back to Bhubaneswar.

Company with the Family Members

The task of being the eldest among the brothers and sisters in an Indian family with no parents surviving is not an easy task. When the parents exist, the role of the elder is intellectual and not managerial; the parents manage the resource allocation and take responsibility for it. When the brothers and sisters are small, the resource allocation could consist of school fees, school dress, books and supplies, pocket money and health related costs. In older age when people have families, housing is an issue and people look for inheritance. In our case, there was no inheritance per se except the house that we built. In addition, there existed a plot of land in Bhubaneswar that was gifted by the Government under a Freedom Fighter Rehabilitation Scheme. The land had been used as a market area in violation of its intended use. It provided small income for the family, but its management had become a problem.

Father never cared for his belongings. I had heard that Hindu law let father's property move over to mother after his death. Abhi had told me that my mother had prepared a signed document commanding equal distribution of all property among the surviving children. He showed the document to me and I was relieved that my tasks would be less onerous. There was a second document signed by mother that suggested a possible allocation of space in the house at Cuttack. Abhi said that we had to hire a lawyer to get the documents registered and make a declaration on behalf of the surviving children. Apu and Lakhi showed up and I showed them the documents. They agreed on the sentiment expressed in the document. I needed to show the document to two more brothers, one who lived at the Cuttack house and another one living in the US. Since it was a signed document by mother, I needed to act on it to accomplish the desired distribution and allocation. I thanked Abhi for his timely work and asked him to check on a lawyer.

The bride and groom left for Lucknow in the evening train. A contingent from the bride's family including the parents would board train in the morning. The question came up regarding my residence the next day and if I should move to Apu's house. I was hesitant. I convinced a young cousin in the family to stick with me the next day. We both would leave the following day morning. I would take the train south on way to Koraput[79] and he would take a flight to go to Bangalore where he worked. Once resolved, I had to schedule my travel. My train ticket was mailed to me on the internet. The cousin friend helped me connect to the internet through a laptop and I confirmed my reservation. I had to get the page printed and carried the hardcopy with me to the train.

It was the time to share stories with the older sisters and their families who had come from Baripada. The oldest sister had been my friend. She had been involved with the Ramakrishna[80]'s teaching and was also a follower Sri Aurobindo[81]. I gave her a copy of my edited book Sri Krishna Yoga and she thanked me. The book was a short summary of the Gita suggesting a prescription on the practice of life. Swami Sarvagatananda, the monk at MIT[82] in Boston, gave a set of lectures in MIT on the doctrine preached by Sri Krishna. I edited the lectures and made into a book after adding new material. A happy man is one

---

[79] *The south west extreme of Orissa state. With hills, forests and waterfalls, the area is spectacularly beautiful.*
[80] *The nineteenth century ascetic saint from Bengal*
[81] *A revolutionary freedom fighter from Bengal turned to be a spiritual master.*
[82] *The reputed technical institution – Massachusetts Institute of Technology*

who has no expectation, is unselfish, chooses his work with discrimination and performs without any mental delusion. You may die in work, but you do not carry regrets. There were discussions in home where people would move the next day. Most would leave and others would relocate to a brother's house. They would linger a few more days and return home.

It was dinner time. I was given my food. The women arranged for a ritualistic meal squatting on the floor. In a big plate, puffed rice was poured liberally and then was mixed with various dishes, chutneys and vegetables. The rice volume decreased as it was wrapped around with various fluid preparations and more rice was added to create a holy bundle. All sisters sat around the plate, and partook rice from the plate like an Afghan[83] meal. Sharing food from the same plate is a celebration of kinship. I wondered how old the culture could be and if it originated in India. Some might think it to be unhygienic, but I thought it was a spectacle of human family. It was not that you break the bread together, but you ate from the same bread. I could not determine if the puffed rice had a special role in this celebration or if it was a substitute for some other grain used earlier. I loved the amity and expressed my delight to the women. I observed my sister also had joined the group and operated as another player in the ritual. I did not ask if men could also join in such a ritual or engage in a separate food communion.

I had papers to check and some books to read. I posted myself on the sofa and watched a bit television to catch up on news. I planned for the next day and went to bed.

---

[83] *Eating from a common plate is an ancestral habit among the hill tribes in Afghanistan.*

DAY-9

SANSKRUTI VIHAR

Wedding event conclusion

The date was July 1, my younger sister Apu's birthday. We had a brother between us, who was sick most of the time. Apu was the baby in the home. She was given more toys than I. Her dresses were better. As children, we notice these. I remember. It is not easy to give equal attention to all children. Children like adults may draw people through their personality. She learned dance with Guru Kelu Charan Mohapatra[84], who was not called "Guru" those days. We called him Kelusir. A nice friendly person with excellent etiquette, I became a pet to him. My sister was too young to take written notes from dictation, I helped. Kelusir would recite them and I would write. I would read them back and he would correct. So were the beginnings of the recording of Odissi dance notes. I did not know that the notes came from the drums to resonate the sound of the feet striking the floor. Eventually Kelusir toured India and

---

[84]*Later awarded Padmavibhusan by the Government of India for his artistic contributions.*

abroad with his students and established Odissi as a major dance routine.

Apu was taking a train to go back to Rourkela[85] where she worked as a physician. She had been there after her graduation from the Medical school since the 70's. She had built a reputation for her good diagnosis. The medical profession gives credit to proper diagnosis; symptoms could look complicated and nonlinear. To sort out the right treatment plan is the key to cure. Unlike the west, the test facilities in the hospitals in India are limited and pathology unreliable. Most readings are intuitive, based on empirical observations. Life expectancy in free India has improved by twenty years since independence. Hovering at sixty-seven years, it is still in the bottom one third in the international scale. My mother spent last years of her life in treatment at the hospital in Rourkela. She spoke highly of the staff there.

All the guests in our wedding reunion party were gradually leaving. Some of them were on way to their place of work, some would linger a few extra days before returning. To live life as a part of society is not easy. One must associate and share life with people. We remember our associations; association builds friendship. Every association needs nurturing. Better is that person who has most friends. Mutual trust builds friendship; any selfishness must go. It is not an easy lesson. Lakhi, the bride and some of the family members were on way to the groom's house for the bride to be received there. They would take the Rajdhani Express, the fast train between Bhubaneswar and Delhi. The trip to Kanpur would take about twenty hours and then they would take a bus to Lucknow. I like the

---

[85] *An industrial city hosting one of the first modern still plants in India.*

inter-State travels and inter-State relationships. India's rich and diverse culture should be explored through travel and association; wedding is a good social channel.

The crowd was getting thin; my Bangalore cousin friend and I remained. I had to leave for Cuttack to attend the practice session of a musical we wanted to stage the following week. My cousin friend was resourceful; he did all my taxi arrangements. The taxi arrived and I left.

Sanskruti Vihar Club

Our Club nucleated in 1962, it was linked to the Chinese invasion to India. India's benevolent high- road non-alignment model of international diplomacy received a jolt and there was confusion. Nehru, the romantic and dreamy leader of India, was distraught. I remember his address on the radio, which was sombre and emotional. India was not prepared for a war; a massive mobilization was required. *Jawan*[86] became a word in the regular vocabulary. We would see off trains and trucks carrying people to the borders for war. In India, most things are done with flowers; and these trains and trucks would be heavily garlanded. Much later, I determined that the garlands were for people who might not return. Nobody kept track how many did not come back. Wars remain impersonal until one encounters it directly through action or through loss of life.

We collected funds for the upkeep of *Jawan*'s families; we would collect sweets and candies to ship to the front lines. Raising funds through cultural presentation was an idea and some of us banded together. The Headmaster in our High School was the mentor and we would do class

---

[86] *A Hindi word for a soldier. Literally means a "young man".*

donations for the cause. The process of singing, dancing, playing musical instruments and doing plays continued and a formal club called Sanskruti Vihar was inaugurated on November 8, 1963. My uncle, Jitu's father, chose the name. The name meant "an abode of culture" in Oriya. The university campus was called Vani Vihar, the abode of knowledge; possibly, it influenced naming. Sri Gokul Chandra Satpathy, the Joint Director of Public Instructions in those days was our President. Our Headmaster Sri Nanda Kishore Rath was the Vice President. I was the Secretary.

Orissa in those days was in the formative stage of her own discovery. The proud Oriya heritage was bottled up by Bengali domination aided by the British. Dominating cultures is possibly a biological activity for the humans. The western culture is now rapidly dominating the east. The domination has subjugation and associated deprivation as its effects. People must relinquish their traditional ways, otherwise they get squeezed economically. Many traditional cultures are dying. Oriya culture could have been wiped out but because of one man standing up. Late Madhusudan Das saw the poverty in the land and called for complete freedom from other dominations. Orissa was declared as an independent State in 1936, but the resource allocation remained poor. Lack of education and reduced opportunity bred corruption. In the '60s, there was a phony competition among the semi-literates; each was defining Oriya culture, as the blind would map out an elephant.

A friend of mine, Chandra, came from a wealthy family that supported traditional Oriya culture in the areas they lived. He took interest in bringing all leading artists of Orissa into forming a team to enact the famous lyrical composition *Indumati* from Kalidasa's *Raghuvamsa* as a dance drama. It was brilliant in concept and exceptional in composition. Sanskruti Vihar was running through my scholarship funds and our estimates in execution were off-track. We staged the production, but were broke and were in massive debt. The pledges did not come through. I hid from people all summer of 1964. We were forgiven because we were teenagers. Eventually we cleared the bills, but learned a critical lesson. We went on a quiet mode for a year; there was political turmoil in the State.

Then in the summer of 1965 came the war with Pakistan. Kashmir has been a prestige issue between India and Pakistan. The Pakistani government had been trying to take over Kashmir under various pretexts. We visited Kashmir through our college team in 1964 and we noticed various military installations on our way. The Kashmir valley is the most beautiful place that nature can create. The green of the grass, the blue of the sky, the silver of the mountains with beautiful people and their animals wait for the poets and lovers of the world. The peace in those mountains was shattered. It must have been hard on people to fight on those rugged terrains. The power seekers have little respect for human life. Alexander, Napoleon and other expeditions had shown the way. For kings and rulers, human life is cheap.

India's Prime Minister Sri Lal Bahadur Sastry died of a stroke after signing the peace document at Tashkent, in modern Uzbekistan. Sri Sastry was a people's man and had no vanity like the one Nehru exhibited. The war and his death drew sympathy from all. We were drawn to the streets; we were committed to help the country. We became a part of the volunteer military trained with rifles and vehicles. Sanskruti Vihar took leadership in organizing poetry meetings, street theatres, lectures, and teach-ins. In the process, we met poets, writers, thinkers, journalists and politicians. Life was getting busy. It was interesting.

Various Oriya writers like Sri Suren Mohanty, Sri Narasingha Mohapatra and Sri Manoranjan Das influenced our thinking to create a forward vision for the State. The profound influence was from Sri Bijoyketan Mangaraj, the famed journalist, who asked us to think of reviving the cultural tradition at *Bali Jatra*. *Bali Jatra* is known as a trade festival in Cuttack held in the month on November. Nobody had told us that it was named so since the sailors left for the Indonesian island of Bali in the historical time. We began to brainstorm what could have been the cultural mode while the sailors left on the adventure trips. We tried to learn Odissi art forms and nuances in Oriya language. We had several sittings with Kabichandra Kalicharan Pattanayak who impressed us that the musical form of drama was essentially an Oriya creation and would need restoration.

We had an accidental meeting in our home with late Sri Dhiren Dash who had just relocated from Bombay to Cuttack. A man of immense creativity, Dhiren Dash had gone into the craft of set design in Bombay and was running a film news magazine in Oriya. He wanted to be in Orissa to raise his young family and was starting a small business. He was a dreamer of discovering the past heritage of Orissa and eventually became a major researcher in Oriya drama and dramatics. He was an intense man; always full of ideas. He suggested that we look into the creations of late poet Baishnaba Pani, who had made enormous contributions to modern musical theatre in Orissa. After reading a few of the scripts, we were sold on the idea.

Early evenings for several weeks, we would go Barabati Fort, where Sri Dash wanted to replay the glory of Orissa. Barabati is a half mile square area surrounded by a thirty feet wide moat that secured the area. The fort was built a thousand years ago, and was demolished by the Islamic invaders five hundred years back. Behind the moat on the front side, there was an elevated land. Dhiren Dash measured it to make the prospective stage. Sri Dash would pound out the grass to let us know what he wanted and how he wanted. We had never worked with a stage Director before. The instructions were lofty and demanding.

The layout was done; a two hundred feet open-air stage with a reflecting pool was the grand idea. We pulled resources; elders in our families helped. Lights, microphones, tents, horses, elephants, chariots, and fireworks were arranged. The production *Biratagodhana Harana* was staged on November 27, 1966. Anybody who was somebody in Oriya folk theatre showed up to help. About fifty thousand people assembled on the other side of the moat to witness the play and the spectacle. My father inaugurated the event with pride in his voice. It was the beginning of a new era in Oriya theatrical arts.

Sanskruti Vihar continued the *Bali Jatra* production in those fancy grounds for many years under the direction of Sri Dash. I participated when I could. Lately the fort has been converted into new housing units. The cultural production is shifted to the dried-out sand areas in the massive Mahanadi River. The sponsorship by the State Administration has reduced the pressure on the Club. Various folk theatre groups are invited from around the State to perform in *Bali Jatra* festival. Sanskruti Vihar players are invited to go to different areas and different States to present their art. Having played his art in Orissa, Sri Dash came to the US in 1991 and lectured on Oriya dramatics at Brown University at Providence, Rhode Island. Unfortunately, I received a call from his son in the winter that year that he succumbed to a massive stroke suddenly. Strokes need not be fatal if immediate help is available. Dhiren Dash was just about sixty. His passing away has been a huge loss to the Orissa theatre arts community.

I arrived at the house of my friend where the Sanskruti Vihar practice session was being held. Nirmal retired as the Director of Public Instructions for the Higher Studies. The house was in an area where the Bengalis have lived for more than a century. Nirmal spoke Bengali at home but was fluent in Oriya when he met us. The famous Oriya poet Radhanath Roy had a similar mix. The father of Oriya prose Fakirmohan Senapati was related to Bengali families. Nirmal was away and we were using his residence. The play we had chosen is *Danabira Harishchandra*[87], the legendary story of the king who was tested by a sage for his veracity and charity. The drama is heart breaking; the story of honest people suffering to keep their word. In Harishchandra's case, it ends in a positive note reinforcing the point that we must live up to our promises in life irrespective of the perceived outcome; a reward could be waiting. It is not a path for the timid.

Narayan directed the play. There were a dozen participants; all did well. In early times, we had male actors playing the female roles; lately the females are hired. The music was well set; I was pleased. I met Baishnab Sahu, one of our old sponsors from the college days. He is a very talented person and is lately busy in doing interpretative lectures on literary and religious topics. He has great interest in music. Chandra, my friend was there. Saroj showed up later. I observed the practice for an hour. We had the

---

[87] *The story goes back to the Vedic times about a king being tested for his righteousness. It could be folk legend.*

community lunch. The lunch was usually brought from the local temple and we shared together. Squatting on the floor in a line and to eat from the leaf plates is a cultural heritage of Oriya teamwork. People cracked jokes and it was a pleasant afternoon.

I met a few other friends. I had a gift for my friend Janaki. I passed it on. I have known Janaki as a volunteer for Sanskruti Vihar from its infancy. He had committed himself to reaching out to people to create resources for the organization. He is a bright man with good literary interest. He is a good friend.

Family Disputes

I left Sanskruti Vihar friends about 4:00 PM and proceeded to my uncle's home. Apparently, the Gita chant the previous day had brought amity among the family members and I wanted to thank them all. My mother was the eldest in their family for the last thirty years of her life. Her older brother passed away first, then my grandfather passed away; now she has passed away. One needed someone to confide oneself in trust; my uncle was alone. All his older siblings were no more. One needed more of trustful friendship, as one got older. The widow aunt could talk to her children and they were getting agitated easily. The bachelor uncle had to keep his emotion internally, he could blow up under stress. Another younger uncle and his wife handled their own lives.

I showed up. We all met in my uncle's office in the house. He had a separate office near the courthouse, but closed it many years ago, when he was needed to take care of the home. To maintain an office needed an assistant; he took many pro bono cases as a part of his idealism to help a weaker party; he lacked resources for an assistant. As he was getting older, he expected others in the family to help him in the upkeep and tidiness of the office; but such support was not dependable. The office had papers piled up on the desk. Fat legal volumes were stacked in the shelves. Everything could take a good solid dusting; massive discarding of papers might not be out of order. For fifteen years or so, he has been involved with a criminal case. Unfortunately, the client had been using him in many other small court cases pro bono.

We all gathered up in his office. I advised Pradeep to help clean the office to have better airflow and make the environment better. My aunt claimed that she swept the floor when occasion demanded. Such statements irritated my uncle. He thought that the papers were stolen from the office, his client had been blaming him and the family members. I learned through my friends that eviction of people from joint family homes was common and the client could be plotting to occupy the house. I brought up my intelligence to the meeting and alerted all that such a plot could be in operation. I had also to state that the widow aunt had a cultural right to stay in the house since she had no place to go. I had seen the widow home in Benares during my trips there. The whole process of the treatment of widows is a sad commentary on Indian culture. I emphasized that we as a family must do different. We must help others who might be evicted through other miscreants.

It is not easy to sort out family problems in a single sitting, but I thought we had candour in our conversation. My uncle raised his voice giving the impression that he was not ready to listen. All people left the room. I felt sad and helpless. I retorted that eviction of the widow aunt must not happen and I left the room. I thought about the erosion of the joint family system through the pressure of life, possibly connected to finance. My aunt received her pension as a widow, but she needed the security of a home. In principle, she could stay with one of her children, but it is unfair that she should be forced to do so. She was also a good friend to the other aunt, who was sick and needed care. It appeared like a drama was being played.

I had more problems to confront. I had a brother who was not in to the father's idealism that we celebrate. Though a bright boy, he has had various grievances all his life; and had gone through various difficult social conditions. He had keen intelligence and was compassionate; but he was not ingrained in the rigor of the family tradition of sacrifice. While many of us had imagined that our Cuttack house would be used for charity for women's education in celebration of my mother, he had been a resistance. I had sent him message to meet me to discuss about setting aside various rooms in the house that can be used as public spaces. He showed up to meet.

A disagreeable younger brother without the parents' presence is a difficult object. After a few short pleasantries, he got back to his list of grievances and his justification why the full house on rent was only an acceptable solution to him. As a son of our father, he seemed resolute. I have hardly spent any time with him after his sixth birthday. I had heard how other families had broken down through family disagreements. I was feeling dismayed that such would be the case in our family. Any erratic person can throw another person out from a joint family home. Litigation was not a solution; it was the beginning of the decay. While I felt that I must try my best not to get broken up, I found that time was not in my favour. Society has not invented any constructive therapy. The flow of time created more dissociation than association. I would still try.

I returned to Bhubaneswar. I had to come to Gita's house for supper. I needed to get my train ticket printed somewhere and get my mobile phone recharged. In Gita's house, I found a muscle therapy assistant working on my brother Sanjoy. He was a smart individual; he monitored Sanjoy's wrist and leg movements through a machine and keeps a chart. There was progress. I was happy to observe his work. I admired Gita's resourcefulness to assist my brother through his difficult period. I asked the Assistant if he could help me in getting a few errands done.

The young man gave me a ride in his motorbike for a journey to the market. In my eagerness to get things done, I had forgotten my immaturity in riding a motorbike. The road as usual was like the foothills of the Himalayas and one had to be extremely careful not to be ejected out. The young person called me back pointing my apparent erratic conduct at the back. Such immaturity in ride possibly caused him stress on the overall balance of the vehicle. I would declare innocence, but he would alert repeatedly. It was a Sunday and late in the evening. Not everything was open; we had to move around a bit. We succeeded in getting our tasks done. I admired the skills of the driver on our return journey. To operate a two-wheel motorized vehicle between occasional ditches of water on uneven terrain is a marvellous feat indeed!

Gita served me a nice hot supper. I spent a little time with Sanjoy. My Bangalore cousin showed up and escorted me in another motorbike ride to Lakhi's house. I had less difficulty this time. Experience helps. We reached the house. It was empty and quiet. We spoke a bit about life in Bangalore and Oriya migration to different cities. He spoke delightfully about the new Jagannatha Temple in Bangalore. I packed my bag for the morning and slept.

DAY - 10

JEYPORE

Train Ride to Vizianagaram

It had been raining since the previous night. These were the monsoons, a welcome to the Indian farmers. Nearly four decades ago, I had worked for Poona Observatory to study India's weather systems. It had the major Forecasting Centre in the country. The weather prediction those days was through the daily synoptic charts. The important forecast was to be climatology-based; a prediction to suggest if the Monsoons would bring enough rains to the right areas in right time. The rainfall pattern can vary from year to year, adding uncertainty to the country's annual economy.

My cousin friend was still sleeping; he must have been exhausted with the weeklong events related to the wedding. I reported to him softly and took off to the road. I had to carefully wade myself to the Railway Station. Automobile rickshaws plied on those side streets and one had to avoid splashes. The drivers were decent; they slowed down when entering the deep ditches, but these could occur every five yards. The technique of finding a rickshaw was to look if it had no passenger sitting and then making hand gesture to gain the driver's attention. It was a skilful exercise.

During the rains, they covered up the cabin completely, so a fully covered up cabin indicated that the rickshaw was occupied. Sometimes, enterprising drivers could signal you to check in case you wanted a ride. The latter happened, and I got a ride. Like the practice, the screens were drawn all around to prevent water coming in. Later, I figured out that the practice was to prevent the splashes entering than to protect against the rain. During the busy times of the day, or near the Railways Station, the rickshaws moved as though in a war zone. One had to witness the expertise in the manoeuvers to believe!

I entered the Railway Station building. It was a busy place. Railway lines were like arteries in the human body. They were networked zigzag to move objects in various directions. There was a big board on the wall displaying the train timings. The scheduled arrival time for the Visakhapatnam Express was 8:15 AM and the departure time 8:30 AM; it did not give a platform number. I stood in a line to ask the Information Officer to get the number of the platform.

Things are dynamic in India; those people are only knowledgeable who use the information. By your question, people can detect that you do not belong in the area; not a good thing to suggest. This apparent profiling has bothered me while living abroad, and I did not wish to be profiled in the land of my birth. I noticed that people at the window might get only a few seconds to ask a question and get an answer. I polished my question in Oriya and delivered it quickly while my turn came at the window. The Officer responded "platform 1" and I was done. Now I had to figure out the geography of Platform 1. I went to a newspaper stall to buy periodicals and asked for the layout of the station. I was relieved to discover that I was indeed on the Platform 1.

It was 8:05. A train entered the platform. I had no reason to think that it was my train because it arrived before its scheduled time. As I knew, trains in India do not come early; sometimes they get late, occasionally severely late. I was supposed to travel Class II/AC and a bogie with that sign was parked right in front of me. There was activity in other areas of the train and not in that bogie. I was watching people. It is always an interesting sight, young business persons instructing their people on the travel; women carrying goods in coarse gunny bags; families traveling together holding each other's hands.

Indian train bogies were partitioned into five feet by six feet areas with a common corridor. A bogie could be a hundred feet in length and collapsible gates to make a large chain could interconnect many bogies. In this class, we had four seats per partition, allowing four persons to sleep if they wished. As I remembered, the first class would have the partitions fashioned with doors as enclosures to create more quiet space.

Mahatma Gandhi[88] was thrown out in South Africa in his effort to join the elite first class. In India, the first class is used by high-end business persons or by political persons. The middle class goes for the Class II AC; AC stands for air-conditioned. The general Class II is not air-conditioned, may have a reserved sleeper compartment,

---

[88]Considered the prime mover in the independence movement to liberate India from the British rule. Now celebrated as the "Father of the Nation" in India.

and an unreserved general. When we were students in college, we used to travel Class III, which is abolished now being converted to Class II unreserved.

The train ran south. I had travelled this way to Hyderabad on my way to Poona several times in the past. To go to Hyderabad, we would come to Khurdha and take a train that would start from Puri. Puri is a pilgrim town where trains originated; they went south to Hyderabad and north to Calcutta. There was no railway line to go to western Orissa. I was going to Jeypore; my train travel would take me to Vijayanagaram and then I would take road transport. An area's economic growth is a function of its connectivity. The places in Orissa were not well connected by rail in general. The Administration at Bhubaneswar remained weak and Orissa's voice in the national scene was also weak. Hopefully, new leaders would emerge from the youth to fight on behalf of the State.

The train brought various vendors to sell breakfast items and tea. I had restriction on outside food; I settled for a cup of tea. The tea was served in thin plastic containers. The liquid was hot; the cup was flimsy; the whole process was unstable. It was unmanageable to the unskilled. Once you hold the cup, you cannot keep it down in a moving train; the hot liquid can spill on you causing burns. It needs expertise to sip tea from that cup. The person in the front seat, a young woman, had her own thermos flask with a detachable cup, which I thought was an appropriate "bring your cup" solution. A man at the window had used a bed sheet to operate as a protection against the hot plastic. I could use my newspaper, but it was too late to make the preparation.

The passenger in the seat in front was from Cuttack. She came from a Bengali family domiciled in Cuttack in an area where I had friends. She was married in a Marwari family in Rajasthan and lived in Jaipur for a while. Her husband was employed in Bangalore and she was on her way there. She could be in her mid-20's and had a sweet face. We had pleasant conversation; she spoke fluent Oriya. I asked how did she land up in Jaipur and she said that they were family friends at Cuttack. I asked if it was difficult to operate in a Marwari household. She said indeed there were restrictions; but she loved them. She must hide her face inside her saree in public, and particularly if the father-in-law was around. I asked if she felt embarrassed with such restrictions. She responded with a jubilant negative. The whole process covering up women's face in various ways is enacted in different manners in different parts of the world. A woman's exposed skin is assumed a distraction in certain beliefs; some conservatives think woman as an object, and some others think woman as a property. Men impose their whims on women. I was happy to hear that she was comfortable with it, not resigned to it.

Apparently, the train had wireless communication; the man at the window was busy on a computer. He had been looking at the screen intently reading the train schedules for an hour. While I was talking to my young friend, the man from the window started pulling a newspaper from my pile. It was not clear if the private property should have protection, but I felt such pulling to be offensive. I told the man if he could ask. He dropped the paper and went back to the window as though he did not know anything about it. He could be in his late 30's, a woman sat at another window; she could be his wife. I tried to gauge the dynamics of the man; it seemed he wanted an engaging activity, looking at the computer screen or looking through the windows were not enough. He could make a friend of me by simply asking me; now he looked away from me. The train was a confined space, he settled to play a computer game with his companion.

The Ticket Collector showed up. The Ticket Collectors are an interesting group of people. Some of the people I knew in college in postgraduate classes moonlighted as Ticket Collectors. I did not know how far they travelled. The Ticket Collectors had a dress that had not changed since the British days. With their black coats and hats, they were a conspicuous presence in the Railway system. They wielded enormous power in the bogie they conduct. Man, is designed to slip in life; some TC's do slip. I had heard that their base salary was low and they compensated with a side income. Though I had not directly bribed a TC, I had been a beneficiary to a seat or a berth in a fully reserved train. There are people in India who are experts in tackling the TC's. I was supposed to show an identification document here if demanded. There was no demand and I did not need to produce my passport. The TC punched my printed electronic receipt and moved on. There was the scope of discretion in the autonomous system.

It was about noon. The train was passing through the vistas of Chilika Lake. From the train, it looked like a large pond. The sight was attractive; there was beauty in water. I asked my friend if she studied Oriya literature; she said that she had some, but had forgotten. She liked English literature; I asked if there are special quotes on water masses in English literature. She politely answered that she had forgotten. She might have thought I was bugging her more than I needed to, or she might have no genuine interest in literature. For a newly married woman, the priorities are certainly different. There could be dreams of family and the future. She could also be missing her home back at Cuttack. I have always thought a woman's life has more responsibilities than the society acknowledges. Motherhood and nurturing a baby has all literature written in the act.

I was proceeding to Jeypore[89] to get a feel of the tribal language. There was no theory behind how words formed in our brain. We seem to repeat what others say. How do others know what they say? Language must start somewhere in human history, but where? The west was not interested in these matters; they would like everyone to modernize. The phonetic content of the rendering a thought had puzzled me enormously.

After Berhampur, I heard Telugu language in the train. I tried to hear and follow. People spoke fast; there was accent. The claim is that Telugu is a Dravidian language while Oriya is Indo-European. These labels are artefacts resulting from some organization attempted by the nineteenth century linguists who were trying to find the origin of the European languages. It is not clear how the state borders are drawn, there are no rivers or mountains to separate. Oriya script has similar rounded curves as Telugu, more seen in Thai and Cambodian. What languages existed in India before the Vedas should be a topic of fundamental research. We must do a lot more to learn how various languages evolved in India. Indus Valley seals might hide a key; people get into fistfights to sort these out since national pride is involved. There are huge gaps in our knowledge in unravelling the history of India.

---

[89] *The principal city in Koraput.*

Some people in the train were served lunch by a caterer who had taken orders before. Eating in the compartment is fun. I loved it as a kid. It has a public atmosphere; the noise in the compartment lulls to murmurs. Some people carry hot pickles and they share with others. Some others bring sweets and they distribute. The lunch operation in the present train was not as massive as the old Howrah-Delhi trains. I was a non-eater because of the restrictions on consuming outside food. Sometimes smell of food at lunchtime can make one feel hungrier, but the smell here was not so appetizing; possibly the food was not fresh.

The station Ichhapuram came and there were vendors with packaged cashews. I thought it was interesting that cashews were sold as snack packages. They were not well dried; I heard later that the product might not be healthy. I had the indication that the economy in Andhra Pradesh was different from Orissa. In another forty-five minutes came Srikakulum, the beginning of the Andhra land. The Andhras are old seafaring people, prosperous and industrious. A considerable part of the northern Andhra Pradesh was a part of Kalinga Empire. The Gangas of Kalinga built the seaside temple of Simhachalam. The Andhra/Kalinga developed the sect of Mahayana Buddhism and the Telugus once ruled the entire the central India. The arts, literature and music sponsored by the Vijayanagara Empire are historic in reach and content.

Laxmi called me on the telephone. He had reached Vizianagaram where I would get down. My train traveller friend would continue her journey. I wished her well in her future life. My arrival at Viziangaram was 2:30 PM local time. The train had been remarkably punctual.

Taxi Travel in the Mountains

Laxmi had brought a taxi from Jeypore. He escorted his sister over from Jeypore to Vizianagaram and she took a train to Bhubaneswar. From travel by train one had to pass the hills and come to the plains to reach Jeypore. Westbound trains went further north, but they were infrequent. They ran on tracks just before the hills begin. A trans-India fast railroad connecting east to west directly would make journey beautiful and interesting. It could get expensive, and was not a priority for a developing country. The people in the hills did not complain much, but lately they were getting violent being incited by the Maoist slogans.

It was about 3:30 PM. Jeypore was about four hours' ride. We started the trip. The driver was a young man, known to Laxmi. Laxmi's family had old estates in Jeypore and he knew various service providers. The taxi operated like a private car with the associated familiarity and fraternity. We passed through Vizianagaram town and proceeded to the highway towards Jeypore. The road had truck traffic, but the condition of the road was good. Occasionally we passed through market areas; otherwise, there were paddy fields on both sides. We went through an area called Gajapatinagaram, which sounded like a satellite of Gajapati district in Orissa. Gaja stood for elephant in Oriya, having a battalion of elephants in the Army, the Oriya kings were called Gajapati; a title that had continued to the modern days. I did not know what Gajapatingaram stood for.

We passed through an area called Salur on the borders of Orissa and Andhra Pradesh. There was a crowd gathered in a distance. Laxmi determined that Monday was the market day for the local farmers. The weekly market called hâma[90] in Oriya is an old tradition. Before physical currency was in use, the farm produce was exchanged in barter; now business persons came to procure. It was a wholesale market; a whole load of vegetables was sold for a very low price. The freshness of the product was excellent, and the prices stunningly low; but one had to collect the entire basket.

A load of cauliflowers could contain a hundred heads; a load of eggplants might be a hundred kilograms. There were trucks around; I had the impression that the businesspersons were waiting for the price to drop still further through non-interaction; a typical business manipulation. There was no union of the farmers, they were independent business units and they operated on cash. There was no Government procurement. With new foreign investment, the procurement might get better since large cold storages to protect the vegetables could become available.

Laxmi and I moved around the market; we located some retail vendors on the other side of the road. Both of us had interest in the exotics; special preparations of food. Most of the wholesale as well as the retail vendors in Salur were women. I did not fully understand their social culture; it looked like an outing for women. Laxmi bargained for vegetables and I enjoyed the conversation. The vendor's voice was kind and affectionate. She made sure that the portions of vegetable were equal; she was motherly in her sincerity. We paid the money and she received it as a businessperson. The whole process was interesting and powerful.

Each vendor had only one product, so one had to

---

[90] *A market place where goods used to be exchanged in barter.*

move around to collect a mix. We went to another woman; she was equally affectionate, kind in her words and business-like in her handling the money. The women had their stuff spread on the ground and there was little competition between them; possibly, they knew that the retail supply was less than the demand. The women were clad in sarees, which were wrapped around their waist and fell up to the knees. Their chests were covered, but it was a one-piece dress. The hair was combed to make a bundle on one side of the face and many of them had beaded ornaments on their necks. The language they spoke was a variation of Oriya; the accent had a nasal tone. Good Oriya is spoken with well-pronounced vowels and they rendered their vowels powerfully. The vowels carry the full expressive capacity; I figured that their affection is a perception of use of the language.

I looked out for male counterparts to hear their voice. There were some men standing, but they did not speak. We found some men wholesalers. I tried to make a conversation; they said that the material was not for sale. Certainly, the men were less cordial, the communication was brief and the voice was brisk. Laxmi moved around looking for more varieties; the driver had also assembled his bags. We carried our bags slowly to the car. The area had gotten crowded with cars, jeeps and other transports; the sun had set. It was about 7 PM; we had spent about an hour and half in that market. We waded our way through the traffic.

I thought about the people around. I did not hear any Telugu, but we were in Andhra Pradesh. Language demarcations in the border areas could be difficult. How about the children and their education, what language would they use? The larger question was whether the life style of the people should change because of modernization. A farmer's lifestyle was free and flexible, should people be allured to the cities to work in the factories? Should they lose their candour and confidence? They were old inhabitants of India, unspoiled through history and aggressions. Should we uproot them by claiming to give them new liberal education or should we design education for their lifestyle? The Christian missionaries were operating to convert some of them as they have done in other countries. Was conversion their only passport to education?

My wife's mother had her farm a hundred and fifty miles to the north of that place. She employed a whole village and they successfully negotiated with the Government for a one-room school for their children. The wife of my wife's younger brother was the teacher and the Principal of the school. The dropout rate was high and the school soon became dysfunctional. The hill people liked the nature and loved the outdoors. They did wonders through a small plot of land. Modern education is too tiring for their children. They lose interest in confined spaces.

India's education system needs massive overhaul. Most go to school to go away from the homeland than work for the land. Rarely people get back to look to their roots. India needs more people who would appreciate their roots. They must be well educated, well rounded and commit themselves to build the country. I wondered how many were driven out as I have been. I wished to work with the natives; I wished to learn the mechanics of how the civilization began.

To reach Jeypore we had to cross the Eastern Ghats, the mountain road that wound its way for about sixty miles. The mountains were not high, there were no tunnels.

We went around the mountains in a spiral path up and down. We ascended the mountains about 8 PM; there was traffic from the opposite direction. The roads were not particularly good. Like other roads in Orissa, the maintenance was poor. This contrasted to the section in Andhra Pradesh earlier. The old King of Jeypore built the road for the convenience of his subjects. The driver seemed to know the road, I felt a bit insecure with the acute turns and the bad road condition. We struggled. After a while, I saw lights down the valley. It looked beautiful, like a resort in the wilderness. Descent from the mountains needs care. We saw some broken-down cars on wayside; the breakdown in those areas could take several days to recover.

Laxmi had arranged for me to stay at a local hotel, called Hotel Krishna. We went there and I checked in. I went to the room to take a wash. There was no water; the plumbing did not work. Plumbing in hotels in India is a problem occasionally. People take a plumber's task in an amateurish way. Oriya plumbers have left the State and had flooded the country. They had monopoly of plumbing jobs in all major cities. There was no plumber left in Orissa itself! The management changed me to a different room that had water. Laxmi did not look as tired, he always maintained an even personality.

We left the hotel to go to Laxmi's house. The town was spread out; the residential sections were away from the Town Centre. We passed by certain areas that Laxmi said belonged to his aunt's family. The father's brothers apparently had a joint family as I had witnessed in the earlier Baripada community. Laxmi's younger brother Nrusingha lived in the ancestral house. It was a renovated Estate house, well built with a front courtyard. We were greeted by Nrusingha and Laxmi's wife Sudipa. Nrusigha's wife had gone away on a wedding. He had two children, a boy and a girl; both were in high school.

Sudipa served us food. She is a good cook. The food was more grain oriented with fresh spices. There was a stylistic difference from Cuttack, there were more root vegetables with spices. I had a good meal. We talked a bit about life in the mountains. Ancestral family living has a different ambience; pictures, furniture, design have heirloom quality. I talked with the children about their education and schooling. The son was on a wheel chair through a disability, but appeared extremely sharp and knowledgeable on the computers. The sister was a great company to him. Nrusingha drove me back to my hotel.

DAY-11

SIGHTSEEING AT JEYPORE

Gupteswar Caves

We always get up earlier than usual in a new place. Furnished with a bed, a TV and a desk, the hotel room was spacious. There was a balcony but another building blocked the view. Getting up in a new place always gave a strange feeling; the feeling could be stranger if one did not have a full plan ready. I depended on Laxmi for the schedule and plan. I had been to the neighbouring Kalahandi[91] area before. I was visiting an organization that was engaged in literacy campaigns. The year was 1991; the place was Khariar Road. A Telugu social worker Sri Swamy led the organization called Viswas. Young volunteers would go in bicycles to villages with placards. There they would do short plays to help people understand the merits of education. I had observed then that women were more interested than men; women want to know health habits. Women took their responsibility as mothers seriously; it could be a natural gift.

---

[91] *A drought-prone area highlighted by starvation deaths. An area possibly inhabited from prehistoric times.*

Various Missionary organizations had gotten active in literacy campaigns. Sometimes literacy is confused with uprooting people from their culture and language. I did not think much about the danger when I was younger. Lately I have felt each person carries a part of human history and each person is important in his or her own way. Human beings can learn multiple languages. A language at birth and childhood is the signature to one's personality. Language is an energy that drives a person. Without language, the man is soulless, dull. You need your language to think; thinking makes you the person you are. Occupation to make a living different from the tradition tries to erase the local language. People say they sacrifice language to gain food; I believe they just withdraw from their personality through such sacrifice. Cultural invasion in the world is rampant; we must create ways to protect all cultures and not run over them.

I turned on the TV; it was piping the pre-recorded programs in Oriya. I did not know if the efforts were made to highlight the local language and culture. Tribal languages are oral; they have no script. Lately there was a thrust that a language needed a script to compose itself. I disagreed with such assertion. Human expression is a sound that is biologically produced. The speech reflected the emotional state of the human being and such pitch could be independent of culture. We needed more research into these areas. To spread education in a country like India was not easy. Not many teachers are skilled in multiple languages to come to teach in the remote areas. Some of the local boys and girls did go outside for education, but it becomes a one-way trip. They might return occasionally to get married or to visit; rarely to work with people.

Laxmi called. He said that he would be delayed by

an hour. I fetched a cup of tea and scanned the newspapers. Not much local news; I was interested in the events on the hills, no one reports. The paper had many pages of Government notices, possibly not relevant for the area. A small-town newspaper to cover the local events would be useful. It needed an entrepreneur to launch; public information on the roads, events and activities was necessary for an active society. I was only observing; it needed work. I supported the Kondhs of Niyamgiri to protect their hills against mining. I expected news on other mining activities. This area was rich in minerals. Forest removal had disastrous effect on the local climate, the cleared areas created an imbalance in the local radiation. The rainfall could drop. The Government must monitor.

I got ready and went downstairs. I meet the Manager of the hotel, a Telugu speaking man who had recently moved to the town. He had two children; they went to Telugu schools. The Manager had an Assistant and he was Oriya speaking; his family moved there three generations back. I asked them about the business climate in town. They were not very enthusiastic. None of them had been to Bhubaneswar or any of the areas in the coast. Their operation was with the south in Andhra Pradesh and occasionally to the west in neighbouring areas of Chhattisgarh.

Laxmi and the driver showed up. We would go to the Gupteswar Cave temple at the border of Orissa and Chhattisgarh. It was about a forty-mile ride. We went in a westerly direction and came across the big Jagannathasagar Lake. It was a large man-made reservoir made by the King to create a water source for the area. It could be a quarter of mile on one side and half a mile on the other, not so well maintained. The roads seemed good, less bumps. We were out of the town in about ten minutes.

The highway was paved; there was not much traffic on the road. The side marshes had water-lily areas. The flowers were taken away for the temples. We saw large stretch of paddy fields on both sides. New paddy was sown anticipating the rains. Separation into the small saplings and creation of evenly spaced rows were required. It is a skilled exercise. The new saplings like to sit in water. Late archaeology suggests that the cultivation of paddy might have originated in some of these areas of the east. It is a natural product to the area.

After about an hour or so, we turned into another road. I saw a burnt-out house on the right. Laxmi said the extremist rebels had ambushed the police outpost. Apparently, the rebels moved in those forests freely; the villagers were coerced to support them. We did not see a single police vehicle of any kind over the whole distance. Now we were entering still denser forests. We might be the only car in the entire area. Possibly people visited the shrine late in the day. We saw another sign towards a reserved forest and the sign for Gupteswar Caves, our destination.

The forest here was green and serene. There were dense broad leaf trees on both sides. A narrow-paved road passed by through the clearance. It felt like a trail very like the elephant forest in Daspalla. After going a few miles in, we stopped at a makeshift road side shrine. Here we were required to offer twigs of leaves. There was a more developed structure off the road; this is the shrine of *Banadurgâ*[92], worshipped in her divine form as *Dâlkhâi*. The deity presided over the forest. There were a few tribal

---

[92] *Meaning the "goddess of the forest", another manifestation of the divine Devî.*

women selling freshly plucked twigs of a special kind from the forest. I should have examined why this twig was chosen as an offering. It was not clear how the candid and open smiles of village women could create a credible business venture.

The road ended at a canyon with a river below. The river gorges through the huge boulders in the north. This was at the foot of the cave shrine. The scene was beautiful with well-made wide steps leading to the water. We went down the steps. There could be fifty of them. The place had been inhabited from very ancient times. The habitation of people in India is not well studied; there is reason to believe that people trekked from the west through the Narmada River and then descended south. These are old areas of human habitation; the home of the first language and music. The new India has huge tasks ahead to explore her heritage.

We lowered our feet in the river water and splashed some water in our face. Touching natural water anywhere is a fulfilling experience; we seem to be longing for it. There is a spiritual communion. Some people were sprinkling water on their head; we also did. Now we had to climb the steps back, which was not very easy. After reaching the road, we bought some coconuts and flowers to offer our prayers at Sri Gupteswar. The vendors were all local women and they seemed to have good business sense. Laxmi appeared to be a good observant of the local rituals. There were massive steps to go to the top of the hill, possibly a hundred of them. The Cave and the Temple were at the top of the hill. We could see the flag on the Temple from below.

There were good stainless steel handrails going zigzag to the top. It appeared to have been done through the King's patronage; well made. We climbed the steps; every ten steps there was a landing. The landing was made to be an aid for the aged and infirm people. We reached the top. There was a room with a big bell hanging from the ceiling and there was a medium sized Nandi statue that was posted on a waist high pedestal. Nandi is a bull and is Shiva's ride. A resting Nandi indicates that Shiva is at home. It is possible that bullock is the most primitive domesticated animal and Shiva had the attribute of friendliness to animals.

Laxmi rang the bell; the noise was interesting on the hilltop. A person guided us to a door on the side that had steps to go down. We went down a level and then there were steps to go to the Cave where Shiva appeared as a *Linga*. *Linga* worship is an old ritual in India. In the geological formations, an evolving rock of any kind could bring attention and the *Linga* as a rock has such organic element of slow geologic evolution associated with it.

The Himalayas itself rose a couple of inches every decade; but an isolated rock gaining height could be considered unusual. In a more spiritual sense, to create an evolving rock needs a huge amount of statistical likelihood and is worth the notice. The land around such areas could get soft and other natural phenomena could appear in the form of special trees, herbal forests or spring water resources.

We reached the Cave and the *Linga*. A brass railing partition with a priest sitting on the other side barricaded it. Laxmi passed on our coconut and flowers, we lighted our lamps on the side platform; the priest muttered a few words not in a very clear manner. He broke the coconut on the side stone. Coconut is a ritualistic offering. Breaking a coconut helps one to gain assurance that some of the possible problems ahead could be averted.

Coconut is a tough nut, its breaking before the Lord was symbolic that the Lord had granted divine help that would enable the devotee to break up and dissolve his/her problems in life. It is a function of faith; faith brings conviction and determination in life. Some interpret the breaking of coconut as a self-admission of breaking one's own ego before the Lord thus begging divine surrender. Coconut water is organic and I wondered about the clean-up of the place. Cleaning of the shrines from the organic waste was a huge logistic problem, particularly when some people could get fanatic about breaking massive amounts of coconuts.

Descent from the Cave was easy. We met two other people who had also come from Jeypore. They were business associates and visited the Temple periodically. They were younger; they ran down the steps quickly. In my case, I had to negotiate the steps with my glasses. A man and his son were also on the return trek. In Hindu faith one needs be physically present to perform a ritual, there are no absentee prayers. I did not ask them about their visit, but observed that the boy was careful and diligent in taking his steps down. A Temple visit is expected to teach us concentration of thought, sincerity and diligence.

We were on our trip back. We stopped by at *Dâlkhâi Banadurgâ* Temple again, this time we had to visit the shrine and to offer the twig bundles there. A bare bodied man was sitting in front the shrine; he got up to collect the twigs. There were five stone pieces set up as deities on a small platform, there was a cloth chandelier hanging from the ceiling along with a long rope bell. I asked the man about the worship service for the deity and if he would offer a service. He said his name was Dora Sabara and he offered ducks and chickens in servicing the deity. He showed me a curved knife and a hole on the floor below where the offering is executed. He said that the Devi would appear in a vision to tell him what the offering should be and then the desired offering was solicited. I was curious. I asked if he would offer some cash in lieu of a bird. He looked at me and then sat down in front of the deities with wide stare towards the middle.

He pulled the rope tied to the bell towards him and went on ringing the bell while staring at the deity. Minutes passed, many other people flocked around to offer their twigs. I felt uncomfortable that I had switched him into a never-ending chatter of the bell. After about twenty minutes he stopped. He took some cooked rice from a covered utensil, and placed a fistful of cooked rice on each of the stones separately. Then he offered flowers to them. Finally, he looked at me, and said that Devi was "pleased" and communicated her pleasure to him. His statement might sound vain, but his single- minded stare for the prolonged period was not vain. For the period, he seemed to be communicating to a living spirit; so, it appeared.

Jeypore Wedding Reception

We retraced our path from Gupteswar and reached Jeypore. We were supposed to be in a wedding reception for lunch. Suddenly there was heavy traffic and we were not able to proceed towards the reception hall. The driver took permission from Laxmi to approach from the reverse direction. Here it was not much different, except we could move in. There were vehicles of various kinds blocking the road; all were courteous, but all were stuck. We decided to park the car at a distance. We walked up. While walking, I came to realize why people preferred to be dropped off directly at the hall. The roads had various mud pits in them and one needed care. We reached the location in about a hundred yards. We entered a compound.

From the number of vehicles and the traffic, it appeared that the event was the only talk in town. The families were entrenched for centuries and they had business relationships. I liked the old-world fraternity. Unlike the evening reception at Bhubaneswar, the daytime reception was more business-like. People could linger longer; distant people would show up. I had not seen a single gas pump or a car repair shop so far, so I was not prepared for the avalanche of vehicles. I did not understand the fabric of life in the town. Nobody seemed to be stuck or showed concern regarding the transports. Was it a triumph of the indigenous technology or that of brilliant maintenance?

A small walkway led to a receiving porch. We met the groom there. He was a cousin to Laxmi and was a local businessperson. His father was around. They greeted us. Laxmi introduced me; they expressed gratitude that we showed up. We entered a big hall where chairs were set up around the wall; they were occupied. The women were going to another room, which hosted the bride. We met Sudipa, who escorted us to the food area. Food was served in the next hall. We entered the hall and I found some objects scattered on the floor. Their density was high and they looked to me as small objects stuck to the floor. Laxmi told me that the practice was to drop the bones after eating the meat away. From the scattered density, I realized that we were late. I was given a plate with my vegetarian choice and we escaped the room to the other less chaotic room.

Laxmi and I sat in a group with Sudipa and a few other women. A group of elderly people sat on a side; others were seated at random. After food, we were introduced with the elders and I chatted a bit. One of them was related to the Buxipatra family. I knew the elder of the brothers with my father. Harishchandra Buxipatra became a Minister in an Orissa cabinet and has passed away. They were a large family, but not politically active any more. I had always wondered if activism was an opportunity or if it was a call for duty. The area certainly needed huge progressive leadership.

Chhattisgarh Waterfalls

Laxmi had planned to visit the waterfalls across the State border in Chhattisgarh State. Sudipa joined us in the trip. We walked up to the car and summoned the driver. We recovered from the town and hit the highway. It was well paved and wide. It led to the border between Orissa and Chhattisgarh. We reached the border in about an hour and there were some commercial check gates there to clear as a protocol in entering a new state. All drivers registered while crossing the border. The taxi drivers needed license to use the road. The area across the border was the old tribal kingdom of Bastar, which was ruled earlier by a popular Oriya king. He was protective of his people and his area. He was killed by police action that resulted in a popular uprising. This area was extremely fertile. It needed nurturing. Lately it had become the hotbed for recruiting the extremist gorillas.

This was Valmiki's Dandakaranya[93]. Panchavati was about eight hundred miles to the west. It was not known if people traveled between these areas in old days. It was the Deccan plateau, the southern side of the Vindhya Mountains.

---

[93] *The forest where the prince Rama was exiled through the story in the Ramayana.*

The houses looked neat; there was an air of prosperity in the area. We asked for directions to the waterfall and proceeded. We reached the beautiful site of Teerathgarh waterfall about 5 PM. Water cascaded about a hundred feet through intermediate steps and flowed out downstream to the forest. There were steps to go down. There was a temple at the base. It would have been an interesting trip to go there, but we did not have time. We took tea at the snack stall and proceeded towards another waterfall.

We got back to the highway and proceeded in the northerly direction. The road now was not so good. It took us about two hours to reach the new place. It was already dark, but the area was illuminated. Then we saw the huge Chitrakote waterfalls. The width of the drop could be several hundred feet though the height could be less than a hundred feet. The Park Service has created a garden and illuminated the entire area. I appreciated the effort. Waterfalls present grandeur of nature; they never grow old. Man, has a stronger connection to massive water flows.

We went up to the market area and sat down at a café. The shop sold ice cream and we took a treat. Our plan was to go to Jagdalpur to visit the shrine of Goddess *Danteswari*[94] in town and then return. It was about 8 PM and we proceeded to Jagdalpur. The original *Danteswari* temple was in a large complex northward. It was one of the foremost Shakti temples in India. There was an old legend that various limbs of the primordial mother Goddess called *Sati* was scattered over the Indian land; the tooth happened to land at the site where the *Danteswari* Temple is situated. *Danta* in Indian Language means "tooth". The temple is a popular site of Devi worship.

---

[94] *Another representation of Devî.*

We went towards the palace where the town temple was located. There was a big open space in front and we parked easily. Men and women had separate areas in the Temple; the priest distributed flowers and red vermilion to all. It was the time for *Arati*; the special moment when the deity is invoked by public prayers. Everybody was singing a prayer in Hindi; which sounded melodious. I compared the present site to that with Dora Sabara's *Banadurgâ*. Both events sought communion with the supernatural, both perhaps provided the experience of such communion. I did the ritual in the Temple, but do believe that the communion is not a transient event; the deity looks at us even though we may not be looking at her at other times.

More people were coming in. Possibly everyone in town visited the Temple before going home for the evening; they have faith in the deity. We debated if it would be a good idea to take some food before returning. The driver thought it might not be safe if we got late; so, we decided to return to Jeypore and think of food there. We reached Jeypore safely; it was 11:30 in the night. Instead of searching for food, I suggested to skip and reconvene in the morning.

DAY - 12

RETURN TO BHUBANESWAR

Borra Caves

I learned the importance of Jeypore in Orissa. It was part of the old Kalinga Empire and the history went back thousands of years. It was the largest town in Dandakaranya situated in a valley surrounded by the mountains. I could see the young children walking to the school and remembered that my wife had her primary education in the town. The children had put on western type uniforms and were possibly going to a Missionary school. The Jesuits had worked on the mountain alleys for a long period to help spread education which had meant to them the promotion of English. Some of the Jesuits were also prominent scholars in the local language and made efforts to integrate with the local public. Usurping people's culture is an age-old adventure by the human beings. We feel good if others can follow us.

Some local king had thought that he could convert the valley, build it up like Kashmir in north. He had moved to create the three hundred acre Jagannathasagara Lake in the area. Some of the kings in olden days did harbour fancy ideas to express their eccentricity and egotism. Water was a good resource; it could be utilized properly. An artificial water reservoir needed maintenance; it required wealth in the community to maintain it. The Government could help, but they did not seem to be interested in these remote parts of the State. There was a new train connection from Jagdalpur to Bhubaneswar; it slowly trekked in the jungles. It ran parallel to the path we came by, but was slow. Jagannathasagara did not seem like a destination for the well connected.

I was up early; I browsed books. I watched programs in the television. A dozen or more Oriya channels piped recorded music. The television was a popular entertainment and marketing medium. The satellites flood hundreds of channels. The media had become a big business. There were usual corruption allegations on the allocation and licensing of channels. I could see that there was good market for greed and money. Democracy needed sustenance and an honest regulating structure. India was developing her institutions; it could take many more decades. Such corruption in channelling new technology to public was an easy path for the shrewd.

I walked up to the corner room of my friends and asked if they could make a cup of tea. They were happy to be asked. I opened the windows in the room and scanned some of the Oriya magazines I was carrying. To have a cup of tea with new material to read is a basic luxury. The habit of reading morning newspaper was dwindling; people were too busy. Some got news from television or even on the phones. Many others did not care. There could be an argument that how does it matter if one did not know. The assumption in favour of acquainting ourselves with the happenings in the world was to participate in the world as a human being. The planet is one and everything is a part of the planetary family. Our goal could be to play our part of the role for the planet. Sometimes we wish to discover what we can get from the planet; it would be more important to think what we can give to the planet. The planet Earth is our mother.

We were supposed to leave town at 9 AM and would go through the mountains to reach Visakhapatnam by evening; then we would take the night train to Bhubaneswar. I packed my belongings; discarded papers, took a shower, tipped the boys; and descended the stairs. I had a little time to mill around in the lobby. I encouraged the Manager to visit Puri and Bhubaneswar. I encouraged his Assistant to keep his children in school. Clearing up the hotel bill, I took a walk outside. The town was not up yet; I did not fully understand why the business would not start up early. It was possible that the traders were out of town and showed up late. The people probably did not depend too much on the local market. Late rising could be associated with the use of alcohol. A happiness index probably dictated a free lifestyle, active or inactive.

Laxmi and Sudipa showed up, we left. Our driver friend had a one-way trip; he had to find a customer to bring back to Jeypore. They had a Taxi Association which tracked the needs and helped with the bookings for a fee. We left town on road to the mountains, this time we would go on a southerly road to the Araku Mountain and visit the famous Borra caves. In an hour or so, we reached Sunabeda, the industrial site that produced MIG aircraft engines for the Indian Air Force. It was a factory established in Soviet collaboration. India had tilted considerably to the Soviet Union after being attacked by China. Trouble with Pakistan followed, provoked by a confrontational diplomacy of the United States. The help of Soviet Union in post-independence India was considerable.

We saw the tall fence of the factory in the distance. There were no other industrial zones. Capital investment needed infrastructure; the MIG factory had not drawn the capital it should have. Similiguda was the next town; the driver was familiar with a store. We stopped by for breakfast. We got good South Indian style breakfast food, nice and warm. Araku was a beautiful valley tucked amidst green mountains. The roads were well kept; they looked being maintained with markings and stripes. The Andhra roads are better- kept than those in Orissa are. There were widened areas at different locations for view. We stopped by. The forests produce the special *jambu* fruit made famous through the Valmiki's *sabari*[95]. Women were selling the fruit in baskets at those viewing stations, but we did not get attracted. We could not consume them without proper cleaning, nor could we carry them for onward travel. They looked attractive, rich in iron. There were peanut vendors who sold peanuts in shells. We bought some; they were smaller and softer than the American peanuts.

We continued travel on the mountain road for a couple of hours. The traffic was not heavy; the road was wide for two-way traffic. There were no trucks on the roads, only four-wheel vehicles and cars. The other road from Vizianagaram was busier. We reached Borra Caves, carved inside the mountain that was discovered by a cowherd boy when his cow fell through the hole. The cow fell forty feet inside but was not injured; this made the claim that Caves possessed supernatural powers. A pilgrim center was born.

---

[95] *The tribal woman made famous through Valmik's writing demonstrating her righteousness and affection.*

The area around had been cleared off the trees and shrubs. A river could be seen underneath. The river flowed through the Caves and water made the Caves through long years of breaking the rocks in geological time.

There were about fifty steps to go down to the Caves; the steps were clean and swept. There were other people visiting. I liked the civic sense of people; they followed a line, not too noisy, appeared disciplined. Once you were inside the Caves, there was a resting place where young men with flashlights waited for the visitor. They were guides to the Caves and could be hired to give a tour. The Caves though looking like a single formation are an ensemble of many connected Caves; sometimes the passage could be very narrow. Water has the amazing property of flowing through whatever opening it finds and then cracking it. All undulations on the surface of the earth are due to water. All poetry and human emotions are connected to the mechanics of water on earth.

We were now equipped with our guide, a young man in his twenties clad with semi-clean trousers and a dark tee shirt. He had the asset of a powerful flashlight and familiarity of the passages. In strange places, one needed guidance. I thought the person was doing a very valuable service. In the back of my mind, I thought about the person's economics. Many people in the world in his age group waited on others to make a living. Such jobs gave independence but not an income to be secure. In the west, tipping was expected to be an added source of income. In India, tipping was only done on the menial tasks, a legacy from the British days. Guiding in the Caves is taken as a white-collar job. This culture should change.

We descended inside the Caves. There could be a hundred steps with railings for support. After getting to a landing below, we saw a small *Linga* shrine in a corner, the usual wonder of an Indian to connect supernatural to unusual formations. The guide now threw light on the ceiling and we saw massive formation of stalactites frozen in time. The work of natural art in marble was a handicraft of water. Gravity had its share in guiding water. Our friend guided light to an area that looked like a sage's face with beard, a good poetic imagination. Human beings think that nature talks in the shape of objects we relate. Various ice deposits on windows in the west are occasionally are confused with the image of Virgin Mary. It is not clear how much marketing is involved in letting people believe in such patterns. Human beings are always vulnerable to an object of hope.

We saw several more formations; these were large and covered whole walls. The guide had his stories on the patterns to create a sense of connection to known historic or literary contexts. We proceeded to see the narrow Gosthani River that flowed through the caves. Narrow passageways connected several caves having different kind of geographic formations. We were told that the caves were lighted on special occasions with various coloured lights to bring out the grandeur of the formations. Inside there was another *Linga* shrine with a thirty-step ride to a platform. We saw a priest here; who was busy in wishing for the visitors who reached. Visitors rewarded him for his religious service. I thought such arbitrary allocation of space to faith related activity was unnecessary and unhelpful. The Caves were leased to private parties for maintenance and they could sublease space for some other restricted purpose.

After spending about an hour in the Caves, we were ready to get back. We rode the steps back, thanked the guide for his service and paid him his rewards. Outside was sunny and very hot. We stopped by at a store selling raw coconuts. Raw coconuts have nice juice inside and sweet flesh. I enjoy them, a luxury reminding of my childhood in Puri with my grandmother. We entered a town called Srungabarapukota, which looked like a trading center. We wished to stop by for lunch and looked for a reasonable place that would be clean.

Road to Visakhapatnam

We took coffee and were back on the road. The driver veered to a neighbouring road leading to a temple for Sri Rama. The temple is known for a large statue of Hanuman. These are lands of Hanuman[96]. Valmiki had associated his character of Hanuman to the area. Here people worshipped the character. I had heard that special events are held in honour of Hanuman. The temple was built by a private Trust. *Hanumanchalisa*[97] was scripted in a marbled panel. I and our driver friend recited together. *Hanumanchalisa* recitation keeps accidents at bay. The temple had a small gift shop; we bought a few gift items.

The road passed through busy towns; it had gained width. The stores on each side were on solid concrete foundations, well done. The traffic was fairly organized with a barrier between the ingoing and outgoing lanes. Some towns also had traffic lights. We were in satellite townships to Visakhapatnam. The urban expanse seemed more than fifty kilometers. As traffic slowed, evening broke on us and lights came up on the street, neon lights

---

[96] *A mythical character in Valmik's Ramayana.*
[97] *A lyric of forty stanzas extolling Hanuman written by the saint poet Tulasi Das in sixteenth century.*

on the stores. I saw various Japanese and Korean signs lighted on big boards and on the storefronts. There were automobile stores with large lots, also I saw farming equipment stores. One could see prosperity from the approach; people seemed to be well off. Andhra had managed to recover from the colonial days; Orissa had not.

We reached Visakhapatnam. I knew of a large Oriya population in the town. People worked in the Steel Mill, many in the shipyard. I had stayed two weeks with a few students and volunteers in Yellimanchili, a small village an hour south from Visakhaptnam. That was 1992; we celebrated the fiftieth anniversary of Quit India movement from that village on Aug 9 that year. A group in the village was active in village reconstruction and I had spent time with them. I should visit them again, but opportunity has not come. The famous Nrusingha temple of Seemachalam was just a few miles north. This was a major pilgrim centre for people from South Orissa.

Train to Bhubaneswar

Our train was at 10:30 PM and it was already 8 PM. The interior of the city is always hotter than the countryside. The Visakhapatnam is an industrial city; the railway station reflects the activity in the city. It is large, well-lit and looked clean. Laxmi had some luggage and we managed to carry it all inside the platform onto the waiting room where we would wait for the train. It was a large hall with benches all around and some rows in the middle. There was a television in the corner and a big board stating the train timings on the middle wall. We sat in the corner that had the television and watched some of the local language programming. Laxmi was tired and he stretched himself.

I prepared oranges and apples for our supper and shared with him and Sudipa. There were other families sitting around waiting for different trains. I looked at my papers and tried to plan the schedule for the next day. I called my sister's house to check their arrival back in Bhubaneswar. She was reassuring that all had gone well.

The train showed up on schedule. I had a berth in the neighbouring cabin. Another person asked me if I would switch my berth for his family to be together. I agreed and now I was further away from my group. We had to sleep through the night. The pillow, a bed sheet and a light blanket were provided with each berth. I spread my bed; put my bag next to my pillow for safety. I tried to sleep. The conductor did the checking and then lights were dimmed. It was not bad; the night went easily. I got up about 4 AM. I brushed my teeth and waited for the train to arrive at Bhubaneswar. Others in the train gradually got up. I went and checked with Laxmi and got him up.

We landed on platform 3 and needed to cross an over bridge to get to exit. Laxmi hired a porter to carry the luggage. The porters walk fast. One must catch up with them. We were out of the station quickly. It was about 5 AM in the morning. I did not have the confidence to reach my sister's house without being guided. I suggested that I could drop off Laxmi and Sudipa on my way and that would make it reasonable for me to give a call to my sister by sunrise. We hired a rickshaw and started.

DAY - 13

FATHER'S BOOK RELEASE

Address location

Finding a residential address through one's own rational intuition may not always lead to a solution. In many areas in the US, something like a Washington Street can go through many towns; each town doing its own counting while numbering. In a town like Cuttack, the address is given referring to various landmarks in a broad general area; areas designating themselves as communities. In Bhubaneswar, the town was divided into various sectors and there are house numbers in each sector. Occasionally the numbering could be counter-intuitive and so was the case with my sister's area. In their area of Shailashreevihar, the odd and even house numbers were separated by a five-hundred-yard field through some clerical error in the original nomenclature. The mix had continued for a generation; there was no escape.

I dropped Laxmi and Sudipa at their house and then proceeded to my sister's house. I wanted to be a little late such that I would not disturb anyone before sunrise; I also did not call to take the directions. I thought to smart them out. The rickshaw reached the area, but we did not see our house number. It was like Hanuman looking for Sita in Lanka. One knew that one was close, but one had no clue why the number was not there. The close numbers existed, but my number was missing. I also could not recognize the neighbourhood though it was not dark any more. We had been moving for about fifteen minutes through the lanes. The driver announced that he had to leave to attend to some kids to take them to school. He dropped me off on the road.

Resigned I began my solitary expedition to look for clues, a *Vibhisana*[98], to help me. I did not have luck. I asked some elderly person who was out on a morning walk; he had no idea. I asked a woman who was collecting flowers in the front yard; she expressed inability. Finally, I saw a group of young men in front of a house and one of them told me the story behind the separation of odd and even marked houses. He said I was a half mile away. Feeling desperate, I gave a call to my sister's house to request rescue. Anjan showed up in his scooter in a few minutes and I was retrieved from my failed expedition. Common sense may not always win; one must be aware of the individuality of all circumstances. All events have life.

Having reached the residence, I shared stories with my sister. They had a good reception in Lucknow; they were happy. To complete a wedding successfully is a fair amount of task. In the west, the parents are less involved than in India. Involvement adds closeness and intimacy; the families come to know each other better. The groom's family was relatively well off; everything was cordial. The couple planned to go on a honeymoon trip to Mauritius,

---

[98] *A character in Ramayana, who helped in to rescue a lost Hanuman.*

the island in south Indian Ocean off the African coast. I shared the dates and nuts sweet I had brought from Andhra Pradesh. My sister made a nice cup of tea. We ruminated a bit about my parents and assumed that they could be sending their blessings.

Blessings are an important part of Indian culture. It is a belief system that our work is only a product achieved through a long chain of events and contexts. Each of the objects in the events is helpful to any success we receive. The failures are entirely ours, our miscommunication or misidentification with the factors matter. Parental blessings are the most important parameter leading to success; we work to please them. Parents are our foremost well-wishers and our ultimate protectors. The cosmology of such a system is not fully analysed; but it seems better than any supernatural coming in play. Any power or miracle is embedded into the people who gave us life directly.

Purchasing Gifts

I had run out of money and needed to go the Bank to get cash. I remembered a Government store near the Bank that sold Orissa handicrafts and I wished to stop by there. It had started raining outside. Rains were good for the fields; it was a nuisance in urban living. Mr. Rabi Dash called; he had arranged the book release event in the evening. I requested him if he could bring a copy for me to see. He is a hard- working and devoted individual, a deep spirit of community work runs in his veins. Supporting weavers in Kalahandi by creating livelihood for them and marketing their goods to create employment in Bhubaneswar was not a small task. He was also a writer and an organizer. Orissa needed many such people to pull the society forward.

Rabi Dash showed up. I saw the book; it was well

done. The cover was bright, with a picture of my father. He had those thinking eyes set in his glasses. A man's inner nature is seen through the eyes; our trust and distrust to an individual is an outcome of our eye contact. To look at an object clearly is an indicator of our own truthfulness. Vedas said that our words are meaningful, but such meaning is possibly true when there is eye contact. Yoga says we can communicate without eye contact, but then we see the object internally in our contemplation.

Rabi Dash dropped me off at the Market building near the office of United Commercial Bank, where I had an account. They continued to have difficulties with foreign exchange transactions and dispatched me back to State Bank of India. Work in the Bank was quickly done; my old friend was there, not much had changed. The exchange rate was slightly down. I wanted to return to the Market building to visit Utkalika. I felt more confident since I could see it on the other side. In principle one could walk across, but there was no over bridge or any pedestrian traffic lines. Everyone moved with their vehicles. I hired a rickshaw to take me around there. The Market Building was a hundred-yard stretch of strip mall when it opened in the '60s. The building had a design to blend with the temple architecture of Bhubaneswar. Now the building was covered up with posters and stores had expanded in all directions. The original building was hidden in the noise of new cabins. One had to look to discover.

Utkalika is a good store, carries items of interest from the local artisans. They have a large stoneware collection, mostly Ganesha[99]. Ganesha statue is popular abroad; it is

---

[99] *Sometimes called the elephant-headed god, an icon of learning and good luck in Hinduism.*

popular to plant a Ganesha statue on the entry for decoration! I have not understood the sanctity of the operation. Ganesha is an icon, not a decoration piece. I wished to buy a Devi statue for my home shrine; they did not have one. They had a large handloom collection and a filigree collection. I bought a couple of bed sheets and a few filigree items to give away as gifts. Upstairs they had stitched garments; I bought dresses for my granddaughters and a kurta for me. Earlier I would buy sarees for my wife, but she was not interested in sarees anymore. Sarees need upkeep and maintenance. In the cold climate, we live, sarees are not useful.

Anjan called, he was in the area and wanted to know if I wished to get home. Indeed, I was ready. I needed to take a bit rest and then get prepared for the book release ceremony. He showed up and we got home. Pradeep had shown up. I paid him back the money I owed for my air tickets. We had lunch and pleasantries. It had started raining bad outside. We sat in the balcony. I dozed off.

Book Release Event

The book release event was scheduled at a public hall called Lohia Manch in Shahidnagar. I had thought that I could go over there with Pradeep. The plan did not work; it was raining hard. I would go with Anjan but we must wait for my sister to return from college. I called my friend Golak, if he would like to come. Golak had joined Indian Navy as an officer after finishing college. Last time I had seen him was in Lonavala when he handled INS Shivaji. This was 1970. I would travel with some military friends and visit his ship. This was before the Bangladesh war. Many of our officer friends got deployed in the war. I have not kept track. Golak and I had been talking on phone, but not able to meet. I told him the location of the event; he said he would show up.

I thought about the book. My father wrote in the preface that the book was written during the period 1964 to 1970 when he was confined in jails for various political reasons. I knew when the two volumes did come out, but I did not pay much attention. By reading it now, it seemed that he had been thinking about the development of Oriya language all along and wanted to discover the true diction of the language. Diction of a language is not given; it forms through literature. Diction is the signature of an area; it is the tone of a culture. It carries the melody and the musicality in the expressions of the language. Not everyone would notice it. Nobody teaches us diction. We develop it by hearing; diction carries the voice of the soil.

My father appears obsessed with the proper use of the language in writing. His observations are acute and sharp. To create a scientific commentary from the subjective perception of melody in the language is hard. This was the task my father had undertaken. Oriya has words and these words rhyme. The words are not long or complicated, but are built on metaphors. Events are broken into syllables, and then spoken rhythmically. I love these dynamics of human expression. There is no theory how we create words; people say we have a built-in grammar in us. I think that the built-in grammar is more musical than mechanical. If something is not sweet to hear, it is not a voice. Oriya has its voice, my father searched for it.

After writing the first volume on the practice of the language, he goes into a second volume on the science of the language. Here the description is more interesting. He goes into why a language exists and how we map thoughts into words. He goes into the theory of communication, transfer of information between parties; individuals and machines. He speaks about space applications, encoding, encryption and compression. He gets into these because he believes a language must teach the farmers about the advances in the sciences. The book becomes a challenge to science as to how we can communicate to the huge semi- literate population such that they can be empowered. I always thought him to be a man romanticizing ideas. This tall thinking takes romanticism a further step up. Somebody should think of building a Konarka. All ideas are human. Human beings indeed do big tasks.

Lakhi, Anjan and I proceeded towards the venue. The location was inside a residential area, Anjan chose to park on the road side curb. The location was a two-storey building. These buildings had high walls, remnant of the colonial architecture. Passing through the foyer, we met Rabi Dash. The books were stacked on a table in front of a hall. The hall could be forty feet by thirty feet with an elevated stage at the far end. There were thirty or so people; my friend Nagen was there. I tried to recognize Dr. Debi Patnaik. I was seeing him after about forty years. Dr. Patnaik is an exceptional linguist. Analyzing structure of the language than get stuck with the sounds is the skill of a linguist. I had requested Rabi Dash to get in touch with Dr. Patnaik to write a preface for my father's book. Dr. Patnaik, like my father, was a pioneer in the field.

The discussion centered on what a word was and how it communicated a thought. The research on this topic is the primary part of speech science and such was the discussion in the book. Extending this we can say that language is a tool through which information is transferred. Here we have a catch: how do we make the transfer efficient; what tools do we need to receive the information; how do we know that we are communicating well. My father advocated and Dr. Patnaik endorsed that the only language that we had expertise was our native language learned in our childhood. It had a neurological signature in us. Any other training was only foreign and our delivery would remain incomplete. It was a simple thesis, but a scientific one. The book developed the framework to design tools keeping our native language as the background. This became the science of the language.

Language can be distorted through mixture; this was a common error by the writers though they might not be aware of it. A distorted language failed to communicate. It is a waste. Through hundreds of examples, the book showed the right and wrong use of Oriya language to maintain its readability and musicality. The psychophysics of hearing and perception is an interesting science and the book is novel in its analysis. The examples may appear subjective, but hearing or reading as an action is indeed subjective; the goal is to convey the meaning. Bhatrhari in seventh century AD spoke about such comprehension from the point of view of sound; here we are talking about the use of words such that there is precision in communication.

Rabi Dash made the opening statements. Prof. Tikayat from the Department of Oriya in the University spoke about beauty of the book. Another linguist followed him. Finally, Dr. Patnaik spoke about the preservation of the language. I was called upon to speak a few words and I stressed on the preservation of Oriya nativity and to help reduce the influence of translated literature. My father spoke about this trend in the book. It would be difficult to have one to one translation between various languages since the use of metaphors is cultural. We need to stress the concept translation that would need oversight and editing.

After a vote of thanks, there was slight refreshments and tea. I had been admiring Dr. Patnaik all evening. He had gone in age but his views were crisp. His message was clean. A language has morphology and such morphology is cultural. A whole pool of dialects might sound different, but could belong to the same stock. I requested him if I could visit him later in the evening to talk over some of my ideas on the development of grammar. He kindly agreed and left. My brother escorted me in a car towards their house. I was dropped off on the way to be picked up by Nagen. Finding house in Bhubaneswar was again an old Tantric ritual and one has to solve various riddles. Eventually we reached a house with a big gate. There was a sign warning an attack dog, not a welcome reading in strange areas. After the death of his wife, Dr. Patnaik had been staying with his daughter and son-in-law who are into the entrepreneurial work of curing ailing educational institutions in Orissa.

A man escorted Nagen and me to a corner room on the first floor of the house; Dr. Patnaik greeted us. There was a bed; books and papers were scattered on the bed. There was a glass cabinet in the side with more books. He offered us two chairs, we sat down. He sat on the bed. We talked.

For various reasons, I had been interested in Sanskrit language for the last thirty years. In the beginning, it was purely for learning as a hobby, but then I had been more occupied with the development grammar and the origin of speech. It was amazing to discover that there was no clinical reason for human speech and there was no theory why we speak as organized as we do. Some people thought speech was Darwinian in evolution; man, was endowed with many limbs to manipulate outgoing breath. This did not explain the relation of speech to thinking and the rendering of words to thoughts. Some others thought that speech was an occurrence that happened at a random instant in human history. This hypothesis was ad-hoc and went out in search of a "language gene" which has not been found.

Sanskrit grammarians thought otherwise. Panini was an anatomist; he described what distinct sounds human beings could produce and noted the airflow patterns to produce them. He discovered that the production of sound was only a capability; the trigger of the thought was the driver. This went into metaphysics what made us think; how did a thought enter our mind? Grammarians in the fifth century speculated that a thought was a manifestation of the cosmic consciousness and hence carried complete information of the objects in it. Sound was linked to the comprehension of the object in mind.

While I admired the grammarians, I tend to believe that the sound production was a reaction either to an impulse, driven by an internal or an external stimulus. The stimulus triggered emotion and a grunt sound might come if a threshold was exceeded. The grunts could possibly be associated with the emotions that were detectible. Nobody had done experiment on the relation of sound to emotion and I wished to propose one. I needed Dr. Patnaik's blessing in analysing this line of thinking. We discussed.

He endorsed my line of thinking by giving examples of monosyllabic words in the forest dwelling tribal languages. He supported the single originator theory to the world's languages. He believed that the concepts were rooted in some primitive and fundamental design. He believed in multilingualism and saw a certain amount of overlap among the spoken languages in terms of communicating a thought or a feeling. Multilingualism had a great sociological basis that one need not uproot oneself from the mother tongue to learn any other language. Mother tongue needed to be firmly embedded in training to help create ideas, thoughts and compositions. Learning of other languages was easier with good rooting in the mother tongue.

I had a second question on the origin of the Sanskrit language. While Sanskrit words had cognates in many European languages, it was not straightforward to conclude that the language was imported. The Vedas had many sounds that were different from the European phonemes. The Vedic prosody appeared to be strictly native to India. Even if we accepted certain incursion of people to India, the development of grammar and lyricism would certainly be in India. The question was, how. While the Indus script remained to be deciphered, there was evidence of trade and social interaction between the northern settlers in India and the Tamils in the south. Along with Tamil, other areas in India possibly had their own spoken language patterns, but had not left behind any literature comparable to the Vedas.

Dr. Patnaik did not support or oppose the entry of external people into the Indian land, but he did believe that strong native languages did exist in different parts of India. He believed that the Vedas borrowed words and sounds liberally from these languages. He did not have a theory how the indigenous Indian sounds entered the Vedas and the origin of many words whose etymologies were in dark. Sanskrit was a constructed language, and it could import and export words freely. Recreating the story on the nature of construction was a difficult process. There had not been much analytic work on the topic. The western philologists tried to discover cognates in the western languages and ignored the indigenous words. The analysis by Indian scholars had been weak for lack of resources.

Dr. Patnaik showed me a few books on multilingualism and talked about his passion of preserving the language of the native people. He used the phrase "social justice", a phrase popularized by the Church. In earlier times, Brahmins and Sanskrit had been dominating people's lives denying them the privilege of learning in their native language. Presently English did it with the same deleterious effect. Imposing new language was a tool of subjugation and it had its effect in pacifying people's aspirations in life and society. The world thinkers should consider seriously about the creativity in the society and the techniques of labour management. We homogenize to make management easier; then we take away the endowed capacity of man to sing in his own voice.

We reminisced a bit about our Poona days and recalled some of our acquaintances. He showed me some of the new books published and some new thesis work done by the students in the university. It was getting close to 10 PM. I begged leave. We hugged. Nagen and I were supposed to go to Laxmi's house for dinner. We left in Nagen's motorbike into the coolness of night of the potholed trails. We reached the paved road and sped up to go to the other side of the town. I was an experienced passenger now and knew how to manipulate my support under the centrifugal forces ready to eject me from the perch in the back of the bike. Man, knows how to survive obstacles!

DAY - 14

EVENTS AT CUTTACK

Upanayana

Old India of the Vedas was ritual oriented. Two sets of people were required for the Vedic rituals. One group was that of the priests, who would recite various mantras to invoke different deities to solicit their grace. The second group was that of carpenters and construction people who helped build the ritual platform. Both these activities needed exactness and discipline. The ritual platform was a rendering of celestial maps. The construction needed mathematical and geometrical calculations. The recitation needed absolute concentration in tone, pitch and pronunciation to invoke a deity using one's voice. Disciplined schoolwork was required for these two groups of people. Young children were initiated to the school through vows. This process has developed as a thread ceremony for the priestly families and an initiation ceremony for the artisan families.

After the Brahman theory came into being, the young men and women were initiated for a path called upanayana "to go near (Brahman)" and this has stuck as a major ritual.

With the priests taking control of the society, the ritual was made into a privilege to the priestly families, called Brahmins (*brâhmaGa*). Lately the caste system developed and any privilege became a birth right coming through the father. Our family originating from core conservatism in Puri is wedded to the ritual. The goal is to get children initiated at an early age to a path of discipline and scholarship. My brother Abhi who lives in Canada chose to host the ceremony during his Orissa visit. The ritual is conducted by the mother's brothers through some theological reasoning. Abhi had scheduled to host the ceremony at Cuttack where the boys' uncles lived.

This was my penultimate day of my stay in Orissa. I had to get my laundry done and pack my bag for the return trip. The technique was to do the laundry at home and then send out for ironing. This saved time, but the latter task was not straightforward; there was no scheduled time when the ironing was done. It was a chance process, subject to negotiation. Sometimes no amount of reward could buy the service; this was against the grain of capitalism. I had admired the independence of the professional guild. The service men should make the rules and not the consumers. Now my love stood against me. After trying out through various people in the house, I resigned to the whim of the guild. I settled to fold the clothes myself such that I could pack and get ready.

Lakhi had more rituals to be completed. The handcrafted wedding shrine had to be dismantled and disposed in a running river. This had cosmological significance of the acceptance of time in physical life. Like water in the river, time flowed in one direction, its destination unknown. We accept it and follow the consequences of the flow. The wedding began a new life;

there was hope and aspiration in time. A mother wished good for the child, to get healthy offspring, prosperity and happiness. My sister was busy with her internal musings and was doing the task. Anjan escorted her in the trip outside.

Apu and Basanta showed up. I would take a ride with them to the event at Cuttack. Lakhi and Anjan would come to Cuttack later. It was a regular college day. Lakhi had to go via the college. Teaching work had some flexibility, but she was also the Department Head, hence had some administrative tasks. Basanta was the driver. He grew up in Bhubaneswar; his family owned land in town. After spending some time as a commissioned officer in Air Force, he had spent time in contracting work and presently engaged in large real estate development in their ancestral property. Bhubaneswar had a real estate boom. With rapid growth, the market was speculative. One saw huge construction projects in the stretch of Bhubaneswar-Cuttack highway. Though it was nothing compared to other major urban areas in the country, the land acquisition for construction appeared large. This could affect food production and environment in course of time.

Cuttack was designed as a fort; to go to the inner part of the city was orchestrated to be a hassle. Now with increased population, the hassle had magnified. The roads were circuitous, narrow and slow; the traffic was arbitrary. Somebody said chaos was the nature of life; Cuttack played it well. It was also the place of the most skilled filigree work in the country. Exquisite pieces of artisanship emerged from the age-old settlements. The *Dussehra*[100] time in the

---

[100] *A special festival in the Fall, celebrating the victory of the Devî on the earth.*

town was special. Huge twenty feet high circular backdrops were created with embroidery like metal work in gold or silver. Such sights of splendour are uncommon anywhere else in the world. Cuttack has been proud of her heritage for a thousand years.

By wading our way through, we reached a massive building out in the middle of the town. It was part of a consumer chain mall operating in various parts of India. Stores, restaurants, play rooms and function halls were enclosed in the large setup. There was a large atrium and all stores and spaces were set up around the open space. The building had four floors. My nephews' event was on the fourth floor, which had the function rooms and function halls. We took a glass-cased Hyatt-like elevator overlooking the open atrium space and arrived on the fourth floor. People around escorted us to the room where the event was being hosted.

The uncles had done great planning. A big platform was created; six priests were chanting various Vedic hymns, sometimes together, sometimes in sequence. I had heard some of the chanting before, not all. One boy was seated next to the eldest uncle and my brother handled the second one. Everybody had put on Indian style ceremonial dress, some in raw silk. There were chairs around for people to sit and witness. Some acknowledged my presence in the room and offered me a chair. I sat down to witness the ritual that made an impression on the young person's mind. I did remember my ritual; my grandfather was keen to get it conducted before he passed away. It was a massive affair in our ancestral home near Puri.

From the design of the ritual, the event was an outdoor process since fire sacrifice called *homa* was involved. *Homa* had old cultural origin to teach renunciation of material objects through sacrifice. Some thought that the offering of the organic objects sacrificed was designed to create massive smoke that might affect condensation and rain in an unstable atmosphere. Such artificial cloud seeding might only be accidental with high saturation; it had more to do with the atmospheric conditions than the smoke created. Time had come for the *homa* ritual for my nephews. As the sacrifice materials were put in fire, massive smoke emerged and they moved towards an open window that held an exhaust fan. My two nephews got engulfed in the smoke since they were seated on the path of smoke towards the window. I advised shutting down the fan to reduce the speed of flow but the boys were stuck. Finally, someone rescued them from the smoke and splashed water on their face. It would be interesting to check with the children in their adult life what flash of the episode stayed in their memory.

Hindu rituals have integrity in them but their observance in the modern urban society is a problem. Most rituals need be revised to transform them to deliver the message than invoking animation. Elaborate ritual is a social event, and the available opportunity and time would reduce as we proceed with our new style of living. Reform movement in Hinduism is slow. The priests did immediate customization and called for a break period. Everybody went out to a buffet lunch in the adjacent hall. Many of our other relatives showed up. We had great conversation. It was a crowd of forty or more; my cousins, their children; my uncles and their families; my brother's wife's extended family; and many others. We met, greeted and shared hugs.

After food, we were back in the event room again.

The boys were given their sacred thread and the *Gayatri*[101] mantra. There was a simulation of begging when the students would recite their mantra and receive alms for food. Buddha perfected this *shramana*[102] process in a different manner. A scholar needed less and must be in austerities to appreciate the grace of life. The kids sat on their seats, the uncle administered the mantra. It is said that the mantra was a careful orchestration of Sanskrit syllables the chanting of which can bring peace to the mind. Out of all such mantra compositions, the *Gayatri* was special and possibly the most primitive. It is an invocation to the Sun by offering a prayer to seek intellect from the great Divinity.

Begging ritual was fun. All well-wishers went near the boys and passed on gifts on a plate that each boy held. The boys were expected to say a line in Sanskrit. They did remarkably well. The process was orderly. About a hundred or so people participated in the process. In the olden days, the children were supposed to go away to a teacher's house after the ceremony; lately they did a simulation. The children pretended to walk away, and then were counselled back by their uncles. The ceremony had gravity and playfulness.

My friend Chitta showed up. I had contacted him from the US in my effort to reach out to my classmates. Chitta was a student to my uncle. He was heavily influenced by my uncle's idealism. He had been to the Himalayas and stayed in many monasteries. With his absentmindedness, it had not been possible for him to maintain a marriage.

---

[101] *A vedic chant used to initiate the students into studying the Vedas.*
[102] *Mendicant renunciates who sustain themselves through charity and public begging.*

His family members had also taken advantage of him and had evicted him out. I met him after about fifty years. He looked slim with very little hair; but his mannerism was exactly as he was in school. I loved it, I felt time had stood still. We talked personal matters and spoke philosophy. He said he would not be staying for the supper. I had to go to the Sanskruti Vihar event at a public hall. We prepared to leave.

My uncle came by and passed to me a well-wrapped gift. It was a book gift from Dr. Bishnu who did Gita chanting with me. He had been diligently producing scriptural material in Oriya script for religious undertakings. He had sent his book on the daily rituals. Being a cardiac surgeon, his interest in religious matters was possibly natural, but to translate, interpret and publish was an involved exercise. I admired his effort.

Chitta and I took a rickshaw and left for Satabdi Bhavan where the Sanskruti Vihar event was being held. It was apparently a new Hall and the rickshaw person took us to a Hall that was not what we wanted. After asking various persons we were guided to the location. I continued to think of navigation in the old communities. There is a wide boundary between the known and the unknown. Knowledge grows only by familiarity. Satabdi Bhavan was a Centenary Hall constructed on behalf of the Utkala Sahitya Samaja "Orissa Literary Guild" on their completion of one hundred years. We used to rent their adjacent smaller hall for our events fifty years ago.

Chitta was initiated into yoga discipline. He did not like to meet people. I liked him very much, but he had to leave. I entered the Hall by myself.

Jâtrâ Danabira Harishchandra

Sanskruti Vihar is a friendship organization. Most of the associates go back more than forty years; a few of us go back more than fifty years. Friendship gets stronger with age and there was a bonding among the associates. Many organizations start with good purpose, but wither out in time. Some develop into institutions with protocols and administrative procedures. A few in the world have lingered as voluntary organizations; we were one of them. In such a state, there is a problem of attracting new volunteers since the old culture could prevail. Sanskruti Vihar was in shortage of new workers and the older ones had reached their retirement. The fifty-year Golden Jubilee was a milestone in our cultural life of growing up in Orissa.

Our friend organizers had invited Sri Chaini, the President of Utkala Sahitya Samaja as the guest for the evening. He was a couple of years' junior to us in college. He was a talented writer in Oriya. Sanskruti Vihar owed its first event to the courtesy of Utkal Sahitya Samaja and we wanted to remember. Other members of the organization were gradually assembling. It was always a joyous gathering. I had invited Pandit Mahapatra, the Odissi music doyen from Puri. We waited for his team to arrive. I met my old friends. These meetings were infrequent after I had been abroad. Some of the friends were in their teens when I recruited them, now many were grandfathers. We did not have women members; we had a few mothers who were helping us. They had passed away.

Pandit Mahapatra and his party arrived and we were ready to begin. There was a short speech session with a few of us recanting the journey of the early days and the subsequent travel. The current President, the Vice-President, the Secretary and I spoke on the history of the organization. Sri Chaini presented a discussion on the variations of folk music and oral literature. We had assembled a crowd of more than a hundred people, not bad for an indoor program in the summer. The crowd comprised of our members and their families. Members' families have been our most loyal cheerleaders.

Pandit Mahapatra performed with his troupe. They were five members. Our time was limited and we were unable to do justice to the talents. Odissi has its own style and genre of presentation; it is highly ornamental in its rendering. The lyric is rendered as a story, the music and dance go together. Pure music simulates the ambience of the story through vocal constructs. That is where the skill of the musician is noticed. It needs long years of training and continued practice. The ornamentation is less in voice, but more in rhythm and diction. Pandit Mahapatra was a master and presented his skill masterfully. The Principal of their Music School in Puri also presented a couple of renditions and we wrapped up this segment of the program. Others in the team wished to perform, but we were late.

Danabira Harishchandra was one of the major compositions of folk poet Baishnab Pani. A prominent player in the revival of folk theater in Orissa, Baishnab Pani is credited with dozens of long-play dramas, short-play musicals and farces. Social satire against oppression and exploitation was his thrust behind the poetic compositions. Like any good lyricist, he put music to his lyrics and performed in the productions. A genius of a man, he lived a life of seventy-five years, but in perpetual penury. He would sell out a whole drama for an evening meal. Men of creativity live poor and do not know how to be secure in life. Even after he received his poetic recognition in free

India, he failed to receive subsistence from the Government. He died in misery. Sanskruti Vihar wished to discover and help individuals who worked among people.

Harishchandra is a story from the Mahabharata. It is not clear if the plot was historical; some believe Mahabharata is based on historical facts. Harishchandra story was about a king, who was known for his charity and character and was tested by a sage. Testing was an old Indian tradition; all good acts needed to be tested for the proof of sincerity. The sage made a large plot by which the king became a destitute. He had to sell off his wife and child eventually. To live to his word, he had to work as a menial servant at a cremation ground. His son got bitten by a snake and the mother brought the dead son for cremation. Having no money, she engaged in a conversation with the king and her identity was revealed. At this height of the story, the sage revealed his plot, helped restore the son to life; gave back the kingdom. The story is poignant and is a part of children's story telling in Indian homes.

Baishnab Pani created his own narration of the story for the best dramatic effect to his judgment. The narrative played well among the masses. Narayan had adapted the shorter version and had edited it to make it a two-hour production. There was a live band on stage; the members in the band appeared experienced. The actors were all amateur players in our organization; the queen and the child were the professional actors. Some of the songs were sung by actors on stage and some were done in background with lip-sync. Narayan himself was in the music area ready to pitch in voice when needed. There was a female vocalist assisting him for the female voices. It was a high pitch drama with emotion, pathos and celebration. My lawyer uncle had shown up and he was enjoying the production. I shared my pleasure with a few friends around. The organization showed its strength by producing a play in ten days of preparation time; an accomplishment!

The play ended at about 10:30 PM. We complimented the artists and committed rewards. My younger brother Abhi showed up to invite all for supper. Some of the members were already committed to go to a wedding reception and only a few responded to my brother's invitation. I begged leave of my friends. I gave them a donation to continue the work. They had to plan work for the whole year.

D A Y - 15

RETURN TO DELHI

Departure from Orissa

Family bond is special. It is not clear how the concept of a family developed in human civilization, but a human child is vulnerable to survival and lingers with the parents longer than the other species. While parents provide nurturing, the child needs company, association and playing partners. The first company for a child is his or her brothers and sisters. Occasionally rivalry could develop among the brothers for attention or security, but the relationship between a brother and sister remains sweet until the end of life. My father had great association with his sisters and they adored him. I love my sisters and I believe they like me.

My sister Lakhi had been waiting to have some free time with me. From a little girl, she was, she had developed to be a wife and mother, now a mother-in-law. She taught English, was good at it. She served as the Head of the Department of English in her college. She had dance and voice training, but had not been able to keep them up with the demands in life. She had lyrical rhythm in her ways of handling tasks. She had possibly developed some personal metaphysical views of life like all human beings, but remained private about her views of the future and the events. The loss of our mother three years ago, had been a shock that we had not been able to recover from yet. She was very dear to my mother.

I sat on a sofa in the living room; she sat on a day bed near the wall. We ruminated about our mother. Mother was a source of strength and resilience. She had weathered heavy beatings in life but worked her way with dignity and determination. My sister was more than ten years younger to me and she was not aware of various situations my mother faced early in her life. This was the first time I was discussing with someone about my mother's life and her entry into the world of public life and sacrifice. To support my father on the causes he believed in was the greatest sacrifice my mother could make. She had to find resources to raise her children. It was a story of a woman's courage for a biographer to probe. Having washed clothes of children and then cooking meal for the family, finally go in the afternoon to help other women in the world was a real-life drama that many might not be able to handle. She was keen on women's education and freedom. Her big heart-felt laughter at her 80th birthday told volumes about her triumph in life.

My father was different. He was passionate, intense and reflective. He was keen to actualize experience to write about them, he was a journalist in the true sense of the word. Poverty is not a word, it is a condition in life; exploitation is not a condition, it is an imposition on the poor. Tolstoy created the model. The worldview tallied to the Marxist ideology, and my father romanticized about people's power. India's traditions and institutions were deeply ingrained in the cultural inertia. Peace loving nature allowed people to accept poverty as a part of life. My father's poetry expressed his passion and declared the freedom of man. It was a sight to witness when he recited his own poems in public gatherings. He loved my mother very much, but was helpless in creating wealth. Most people tend towards corrupt methods and he was lonely in his operational strategy. The family members believed in him and they were his dependable support.

We talked about our brothers and sisters. Not everybody has been as lucky as my sisters have been. Some of the brothers were still struggling. I had the tricky task of dividing our inheritance among the brothers and sisters. This was not going to be easy. I sought my sister's help in this effort particularly in view of the younger brothers who had small children. My sister inquired about my family in the US and my son. We needed to get all people connected across the continents. I committed myself to create an extended family mail network to facilitate communication with each other. People were scattered all over India, the US, Canada, the UK and Australia. We should plan a family reunion.

Lakhi was doing a doctoral thesis on the topic of writers of Indian descent living abroad. She talked about her line of research as the writers' view of sociology in Indian context. She also spoke about her own family and the just married daughter. I felt happy that she related her life to larger flow of life in the society. Her younger daughter wanted to be a Company Secretary; my sister wanted to support her. The process was extremely competitive. Then we spoke of her in-laws and I complimented her being a person of grace amidst involved tasks. She was respected for her honesty and sincerity; at the same time, she treaded her path carefully not to cause disharmony. These are difficult traits in modern life.

It was getting late. I had to take a flight in the morning. She guided me to my bed and I quickly went to sleep. I got up at 7 AM and started packing my bags. Akshay, the driver for my other sister, showed up. He had been asked if I needed help to go to the airport. Anjan said that he would drop me off. Akshay was a sincere and diligent individual, looked after various tasks for my older brother-in-law Basanta in Bhubaneswar. He was a family man with two children. I gave a small cash gift for his children.

Our friend Nagen showed up. He had been extremely helpful in my trip. He was supposed to bring me a handloom tablecloth. I received the material and spoke to him. We had breakfast together. He had to go back to work. I told him that we would remain in touch. It was time for me to take a shower and get ready for the flight. I made a few phone calls to Delhi and then prepared to leave. I gave away the remaining Indian currency to my sister and my niece Rini. Young people have uses for cash. I wished Rini luck in her studies and her future.

Anjan, Lakhi and I left for the airport at about 8:45 AM. It was a forty-five-minute ride. The town traffic was relatively easy on a Saturday morning. We breezed through and then we met Laxmi at the entrance to the airport. Laxmi is the most affectionate and the friendliest person one can imagine. He is humble to the core and his humility covers his erudition and insight. We unloaded my luggage from Anjan's car and I begged leave of Anjan and Lakhi. I blessed my sister and hugged Anjan. Leaving is always emotional.

Laxmi helped trolley my luggage over to the airport security entrance. I took leave of him. I admired his friendship and company. We hoped to do joint projects in the future. We hugged each other and I entered the secure area. The airport operations in Bhubaneswar were simpler; there were no lines, less people, less noise. We had to get our luggage scanned and then get the boarding pass. Things happened quickly and I went through the passenger security scan. There was a large hall used as the departure lounge. The airplane was supposed to arrive from Delhi and then take off. I got a cup of coffee and waited.

Looking around I noticed my friend Prashanta Nanda, who was active in Oriya films. We were classmates in Ravenshaw Collegiate. He was recruited into the movies from the school. He made a good name as an actor and lately was busy in directing. The movie industry in Orissa was still in its formative stage; capital investment is small. They made low budget movies for entertainment and quality was not so detailed. I liked him as a friend. He had also dabbled into the Orissa politics being elected to the legislative assembly. I learned that he had changed his political party lately. On this trip, he was going on a tour to Singapore to choose sites for location shooting for a new movie. His producer friend accompanied him. They were a good team.

The flight arrived and the departure was announced. We were guided to a gate on our way to the aircraft. It is not common in India to switch seats at the aircraft. We went to our respective allocations. The plane left punctually.

Lunch with the Nephew's In-Laws

The flight reached Delhi about noon. I had planned to go to Jitu's house to meet Ritu's parents. I felt a special obligation to meet them to offer my sympathy and give them confidence. I did the prepaid taxi and the usual ritual followed. I was directed to a spot and a box-like object rolled in. There was a young driver and he had an assistant. I had not figured out the assistant logic, but it did not bother me. I was at the end of my journey; I had to leave India leaving her with her own mode of operation. Our emotions while entering a place are different than when leaving. When we arrive, we have aspiration and activity. When we leave, we have acceptance and internalization. Life itself is a journey.

  The taxi went in a general direction that I recognized. It had to go to Sultanpur and then look for the house. The house had a number, but the number did not seem to have an order. Various other indices and milestones were required to navigate. We took help from Ritu's father by phone. He guided the driver. The driver proceeded, but failed to find the mosque where we were supposed to make a turn. We circled our way around. Suddenly an elderly man with turban and beard waved at us and I guessed that he could be Ritu's father. He came and greeted me. Then he entered the taxi and escorted us the rest of the way. Possibly the residents in Delhi realize the complexity, but take it easy. Delhi is an old city and these areas were old villages. They are not geared for motor traffic or strange people visiting from faraway lands. I learned that the mosque was hidden beside the stores.

  Sri Singh is a tall upright man, friendly and sincere looking. He did carry the tension of losing the husband of his only daughter, the older of his two children. We negotiated with the taxi if he could come back to pick me up in two hours; the driver refused. He wanted to stay and charge the meter. Sri Singh decided that we let the taxi go and find an alternate transport to get back. I needed to get back to my uncle's residence and then join a few friends for supper. These friends were our old college classmates; I would be meeting some after some forty plus years.

Jitu's building was a four-storey structure with two apartments in each floor. There was a car parked in the front entrance. Several motor bikes parked by the side. We made our way through the parked traffic, and rode the stairs. Sri Singh decided that my bigger bag could stay downstairs in the car, which apparently, he owned. He had his own taxi business while he worked, but now he had retired. Jitu had procured the car. It had cleared off the loan. Jitu's place was on the top floor, the apartment was still under the bank loan. Because of adjustable rates, the bank interest changes every year, causing them stress. For human beings, housing is a necessity, occasionally a luxury. Unlike many other animals, we need a roof, but the need to get a shelter carried the bondage of capital along with it. People get rich by owning land, an early human discovery; so, we have wars and subjugation of people to own land. It is a sad story, not easy to escape!

Ritu's apartment was neat, orderly and comfortable. Sri Singh and I sit in the living room sofa and chair. Ritu's mother was near the kitchen and she greeted me. She was a tall stately woman with strong features, there was a built-in boldness in her eyes. She asked me what food I took for lunch. Unlike our life abroad, a Punjabi lunch is cooked to order, fresh and hot. I said my usual staple of rice, dal and sabji. She went inside the kitchen. Sri Singh described to me the happenings of Jitu's passing away.

Two days before Jitu died, he complained of chest pain, but refused to go to the hospital. He took rest and felt better. Everything seemed normal the next day, but he did not go for any medical checkup. The following day he complained of severe pain and Ritu's parents came by. They advised him to go the hospital right away, but again he refused. He was merely thirty-nine, possibly never thought that he was having a heart stroke. The pain increased in the afternoon. Ritu's father called an ambulance. Jitu was unconscious when the paramedics arrived. They tried to resuscitate him and carried him to the hospital. He passed away on the road.

Sri Singh narrated the events in a matter-of-fact manner and had little emotion in voice. I saw grief in his eyes. The mother would peep out from the kitchen and would add a few details on timing and facts. Both were full of praise to Jitu and said they were blessed to get a person like him as son-in-law. I had thought if they would ask the custom of remarriage, but they were not in that direction. I appreciated their intense liking to my deceased nephew. I committed to carry the message to the family and to do what I could to get the child educated.

The little girl Yasna was nine years old; she was bright, intelligent and good-looking. She showed me her schoolwork from her book bag. She had excellent handwriting and skillful artistic abilities. I loved the girl's manners. I admired her conversational style. I played and joked with her; she responded with her shy smiles and beautiful eye gestures. She attended a private school on the other side of the city. The tuition was expensive. I had not figured out how they would tread their future path, but they had a great child talent in their house. I hoped her path would clear itself in the future. The family seemed committed.

Food was served; nice hot flavourful dishes. Yasna was a regular eater; she, I and Sri Singh ate on a small table. I admired the food quality and appreciated the culture of serving fresh food. With women joining the work force, it was not easy to keep up with the culture. India has many traditional values built on duties, family and health. The urban development clashed with the traditional culture. The country was in a flux now. Most of the old culture might be cleared out in another fifty years. Possibly a hybrid culture could arise. Presently it looked noisy.

Sri Singh had decided that he would drop me off at my uncle's house in Alaknanda. His offer took off an enormous weight from me. I begged leave of Yasna and Jitu's mother-in-law and descended the stairs. Sri Singh guided me to the car and asked me the address. I said the name of Don Bosco High School in the area and he knew where exactly it was. I said that I could guide him to the apartment complex from the school. He said that he knows the apartment complex also. I was in great hands, one who knew the location by citing names.

It was about forty-five minutes' ride and we were in my uncle's house about 4 PM. I invited Sri Singh to come upstairs to meet my uncle. We took the elevator and came up. My uncle opened the door and invited us in. I introduced Sri Singh and they talked in crisp Hindi. My uncle had lived all his life outside Orissa and his Hindi was fluent. I liked it. Sri Singh was a bit reserved, but they had good communication. My aunt served him some sweets and a cup of tea. I was happy that Sri Singh did visit my uncle and appreciated the homeliness.

I had to prepare to go to my next appointment. I escorted Sri Singh down. My next trip into town might not be so smooth. Any unescorted trip is an event of adventure to me!

Old College Friends

I had two more tasks to do in Delhi. One was to meet a dancer Ms. Reela, who has launched a new style of performing Odissi by choreographing the yogic moods into dance. She was the niece of a friend of mine and had been in touch before I left for Orissa. She organized cultural tours and was interested in visiting the USA. The second task was to present myself at an eating-place to meet some of my old college friends who had joined the Indian Civil Service and had retired. Many people of this category worked the final years at Delhi and became residents in the city. There was a sizable population of retired civil servants in Delhi.

Ms. Reela did not have transport and I did not have enough ammunition to find her apartment in Delhi. We mutually cancelled the appointment. That made life a little easier. I sat down with my uncle for an hour and narrated to him about my travels in Orissa. He did not leave Delhi these days and Orissa stories were nostalgic to him. He seemed anxious. He heard with attention. I spoke about my wanderings, the wedding, the events at Cuttack and my interaction with people. My aunt came by and asked if I knew how to get to the site of my dinner. On this tease, I was most vulnerable. I was supposed to go to a place called India International Centre Annex, which was possibly a Club location for the civil servants. We called Seema to advise me on some of the milestones in the area. She was an ever-alert repository of information. Armed with the tips I began adventure into the evening traffic of Delhi. It was summer; there was still some light in the sky. I gathered courage to ride out.

Success of any endeavour in life depended on the company one had. The driver of the rickshaw I took from Alaknanda was the sincerest persons I had met. Possibly all human beings are good, but may not always display their best. Rare are those individuals who are good in all occasions. My driver was one of those rare individuals. I was taken to a building set back more than a hundred yards from the road. He reached there after a couple of wrong turns. I rewarded him for his diligence. There was no one to be seen in the area, only cars parked. I looked at my watch, and it was past our appointed time of 7:30 PM. The building had a security person in the lobby. I felt awkward to be in a private location without an escort. I decided to wait until 8PM in case I arrived at the wrong location. I walked around in the parking lot.

Besides being new to the location, I also had different vulnerability. Gokul was the organizer of the supper. I had memory of him of our college days. We were in college elocution team; we went on college Rover Crew trips. Gokul helped when we had to keep the body of our friend Loknath who committed suicide. I had only an imagination he might be looking; we did not exchange pictures. A man was driven in a car to the parking lot and then he walked towards the gate. He had an Indian kurta and walked briskly. I shouted if he was Gokul. He smiled, came closer and told me that he was not Gokul but he would also join the supper. I felt a Godsend that someone was there, my bifocal had betrayed. I was curious to dig into my memory from the list that was given to me. I asked him in Oriya, and he said he is Subas, another civil servant. I knew Subas in college, but not as well as the others. I did not know that he was coming. He escorted me to the upstairs lounge.

Subas had been active in historical studies and had done a PhD dissertation researching on to the twelfth century Sanskrit poet Jayadeva. He told me about his work in compiling the full text of Jayadeva's composition Geetagovinda. Inspired by his father, he had worked on the project using all his available time to discover the musical renderings of the material. He had finally produced a set of five CD's that contain the complete collection of the twenty-four poems (*astapad*[103]is) of the famous composition. An astapadi was a poem of eight stanzas. Jayadeva's music celebrated the regional tradition of Orissa and Subas was excited about the work. I wanted to hear the music and he committed to pass one on to me.

Gokul showed up at our location. His face looked mature, like mine might look to him. He had the same profile as before. My extrapolation of Gokul to Subas was a total blunder. All of them retain their characteristic features, but our memory of the original features does get feeble in time only to revive by direct sight. Gokul sat next to me and we talked about life and about time past. He was married with two sons, both of whom have done doctoral work and were into information technology work in the US. He served as a senior civil servant and took an early retirement in 1998. Presently he developed his own company on consulting on issues on agricultural production.

Prasanna and Manilal came in together. Prasanna was my old friend from the high school days. He visited the US occasionally and I had met him abroad. He was retired and kept busy as a Consultant to various States and other nations in health-related matters. His older brother was also a civil servant and had visited me when he came to Cambridge in 1990. They were part of a large and accomplished family in Orissa. Prasanna was a short story writer; and had published his stories as books. His work as the Commissioner in Delhi to route the supplies for

---

[103] *A lyric of eight stanzas made famous by the poet Jayadeva.*

distribution during the relief efforts in Orissa was commendable.

Manilal was a year junior to us. Like the rest of my friends, he came to Delhi after graduation in Orissa. He qualified for the Indian Foreign Service. He had served with distinction in Indian Missions in many countries like Nepal, Pakistan, Canada, Russia, Bangladesh, Rumania and Japan. Being a diplomat, he had developed a reserve personality, but lately he had suffered a stroke that paralyzed part of his body. He was slowly recovering, not fully fit. Knowing that we were getting together, he had made himself out of home to be with us. His wife was also a Foreign Service diplomat and she was deeply concerned about his health. Their two children lived abroad.

India International Center was an exclusive Members' Club and I learned that it also had residential accommodation. The Annexe served food and had meeting space for conferences. The serving waiter had outfit style reminding of the old British days. He brought appetizers and peanuts and took the order for drinks. None of us was liquor oriented; we ordered soft drinks. The setting of the room and the conduct was more western than Indian. I had heard that some of the older Indian officers were attempting to be like their British counterparts in taste. The culture had stayed.

It was time for dinner; the dining room was one floor up. We took the stairs; Prasanna escorted Manilal through the elevator. Five of us sat comfortably at a circular table. Another waiter showed up in the company outfit and took our orders. I was a vegetarian and had my food restrictions. It appeared that the management was careful since most guests were current or retired Government officials. There was certainly a hierarchy in people greeting senior people;

there was strong Confucian order of age and experience. Various groups remained self-contained, did not mingle. Possibly mingling across the ranks was considered bad manners in bureaucracy.

I was awed by the cumulative experience of people at my table. They knew the Government inside and out. They had been in position of decision making in crucial areas. The politicians talk; the bureaucrats work, Politicians go corrupt and they pressure the bureaucrats to follow suit. It is very easy to get one's reputation stained; my friends had completed their term without blemish, a remarkable achievement. Now since they were retired, they were free to express their opinion about the politicians. Discussion came to the Orissa politicians, none of the politicians stood out in my friends' views. I had observed the poor state in Orissa during the past two weeks. I listened silently.

My friends were respectful and cordial among themselves. I encouraged them to meet whenever opportunity warranted. We paid the bill and got up. On our way, out we meet Sri N. Mohanty, another retired civil servant. He belonged to an older cadre; he was happy to see me and greeted me. I had met him in Allahabad in the late '50s when my uncle was there. We left the dining area and walked towards the stairs. Prasanna again escorted Manilal through the elevator and we took the steps. We shared hugs. My friends are affectionate. Gokul negotiated with Subas to drop me off on his way home. Everybody bade good night; I left with Subas.

Subas had a driver. He instructed the driver about the direction of our travel. My hint of Don Bosco did not fly well and I called my uncle for help. With guidance; we made our way through and reached my uncle's home. Subas requested me to call him and go via his house the next day on my way to the airport. I agreed. He left bidding me good night. I walked my steps into the apartment complex and took the elevator to my uncle's residence.

It was 10:30 in the night; both uncle and aunt were still up and waiting. Seema had shown up. She visited every Saturday and stayed overnight; a great daughter to take care of the aging parents. It was a remarkable family partnership, I admired. Seema was a nice and competent person. I came by and sat down in the living room. I told them about graduating the tasks of traveling in Delhi and coming back without much problem. I shared my experience of my meeting my old friends. My uncle seemed to know Gokul, Subas and Prasanna in various contexts. I spoke to Seema about her children. We watched news in the television and it was time to go to bed.

DEPARTURE FROM DELHI

Flight to London

This morning was different. It was a Sunday. I did get up in my usual time and made a phone call to my home in the US. Then I called Sandeep in London. My plan was to stop by overnight in London and take the morning flight to Boston. Seema and aunt watched movie in television until pretty late and they were still sleeping. My uncle was up and the tea ritual was in process. The Japanese have made tea drinking as a ceremony; tea operation in my uncle's residence was no less. There was discipline, dignity, solitude and solid engineering skills. I had my share of delight in the cup.

My uncle asked if I would go out for the morning walk. I agreed. We dressed up and went out to the cool morning air. This time we did not take the car; just walked. We crossed the road and entered another apartment complex. Some people were playing badminton in the courtyard. I thought my uncle was showing me another aspect of urban living. Some people there greeted my uncle; he returned the greetings but just proceeded straight. We stopped by at a small garden house. I realized it was a mini canteen. Uncle walked to the window and ordered idlis, which were given in plastic bags. He put them in another bag that he had carried and we were ready to return. Uncle said these idlis were the favorite to Seema and it was an old ritual. I admired the father's love to his daughter.

We returned home. Both my aunt and Seema were up by this time. They were in the living room. Uncle put the bag of idlis on the dining table. I made one more phone call, this time to Biraj in Australia. Biraj was the youngest child of my uncle and the only son. He served as an accounting manager for an auditing company. He had a young son who was twenty years old. Biraj had been helping my uncle and aunt by visiting them almost every quarter. I was speaking to him after twenty years. He picked up the phone. I complimented him for his dutiful work towards his parents. I invited him to visit me in the US and wished him well in his life. He reciprocated in a good brotherly manner.

We all had a good idli breakfast. I gave to my aunt some regional sweets I had brought from Orissa. I packed my bag and was ready to take a shower. It was about 9:30, my taxi was supposed to come at 10:30. I took shower and got dressed. My stay in India was about to conclude. We all sat down and had a bit last minute chat. I received the call from the driver. I was ready to leave. I hugged my aunt, uncle and Seema and told them that I would be in touch and would try to return soon. Uncle escorted me down in the elevator to the taxi. With my luggage loaded, I touched my uncle's feet and begged to leave.

I requested the driver to go via Subas's house. We called him to get the direction. Being satisfied, the taxi was on its way. It went in the direction of Delhi IIT. Subas lived in a rented apartment in the new housing colony there. As usual, the numbers were again mixed up and we came across a huge road block on an apparently one-way street. These arbitrary infrastructure works happened in Delhi without warning. The claim was that Sunday was expected to have low traffic, hence the construction. We overcame the hurdle; but in the process, we bypassed our row for address. Then we went forward and tried reentering from the other side. Suddenly I saw Subas on the road waving. I was relieved. He gave me a packet of material including the CD's that he had created. We shook hands and I left for the airport.

Delhi is a horizontally spread out city, any place to any place can take an hour to reach. In high traffic times, the delay can be enormous. With the new traffic lights, the travel was a bit easy. We reached airport within an hour. Delhi airport was fully modernized. Under the new rule of subtle foreign influence, all the old cultural identities were removed and the building looked like any technology building in a western country. India is known for her cultural artefacts, her subtleties in flooring, walls and the roof. None of that was here; one certainly got a feel that the rules and design are not made by people who knew India's culture. I did not like the noisy atmosphere before, but the style of India needed maintenance and preservation.

I was flying Virgin Atlantic; the lines were already made. I got my luggage booked and obtained the boarding pass. I tried to look for a newspaper stall and there was none. There was a booth saying free newspapers, but the clerk said that it was closed. Stores sold fancy items possibly made in China. There were usual perfume and luggage. I did not see a store selling Indian handicrafts or textiles. There was a food court in the mezzanine level; I thought to try it out. Here one gets Indian lunch along with other international easy dishes. I settled for some north Indian style food just to feel the country before I fly out. Delhi airport had become unusually un-Indian.

There was an announcement to go to the gate for departure. I proceeded to the gate.

Night Halt at London

The journey from Delhi to London was the busiest air travel from India. India had chosen to remain a Commonwealth country and the reward of visiting London by any willing citizen was a privilege used by many. London had always been a shelter for poets, philosophers, radicals and free thinkers. People of Indian origin visited London on business, financial transactions, to join the work force or to pursue studies. Many of the leaders of early India were educated in London and learned the methods to oppose oppression by interacting in English schools. England had a bipolar role towards India; on one hand, it exploited the nation and tried to uproot her culture. On the other, it gave education to her students to help get the English removed from the Indian soil. History has not analyzed who gained more through the English rule in India. India had transformed. She was slowly rediscovering herself back to her roots.

I was flying in an Airbus340/600, a large aircraft full with passengers. I am attracted to the personality of Richard Branson, who is deprived of a high school education but has been a visionary and a successful businessperson. I liked his charisma, a man who appeared to care. The aircraft was well serviced and clean unlike the Air India flights I had taken earlier. I kept my allegiance with Air India having been a part of the family in my early student days, but lately they have become utterly disorganized. There was a theory that the government regulation killed the enterprising Maharaja; now I travelled with the new scarlet maiden painted on the tail. The hospitality and the service were better.

The flight duration was nine hours and thirty-five minutes; out of which I gained five and half hours by traveling west. The arrival time in London was little after 5 PM local time adjusted to the hour of summer Day Light Saving. The flight was in time. The usual picture of Heathrow pass ways and multiple winding glassed walkways had to be overcome to come to the big reception hall and then to wade through. This time I had made friends in Delhi and I see them in the hall.

The line moved. Brown officers showed up and suddenly reoriented the line by realigning the elastic straps, stretching and hooking to poles to make the line. The autonomy of queue management through realignment is an interesting exercise in flow dynamics. I found later that the person was busy in exhibiting his ingenuity at many locations. The calculus of the work in efficiency and time management needed be studied. I lost my friends through this realignment, but I was ahead in the queue. I cleared the passport desk and walked by the customs. I was in that seemingly public space where the whole world assembled to meet people. There were many dresses, many hairdos, many colors and many faces. Human beings are one of the many living species; among human beings we are one among many that are conceived.

I walked around, but did not see my nephew Deepan. Some people looked at me possibly thinking I might fit some description they had come to meet. Deepan was a tall young man, he could not be missed. I walked around more and convinced myself that Deepan was not in the area. I decided to wait in a corner. Twenty minutes passed, no Deepan. I went to a phone booth and tried to call. Nobody picked the phone. I assumed he was probably on his way. I waited. I watched the human drama of hugs, children, anticipations and reunions. Finally, he and Kirti came running. They were stuck in traffic. We gathered luggage and were on our way.

London traffic is clumsy possibly because everything has evolved in time. The town is old. The buildings do show age; they have history. At various intersections, there were big signs of the "Olympics" and "Welcome Athlete" banners. The Olympic event was a business magnet for London and the city waited for the cash flow. There were building constructions around, the road construction was seen every furlong. Deepan knew the road, but his access was blocked by traffic rerouting. Between the two young men, they negotiated, looked for GPS and settled the road. One needed to be street-smart in London.

Through various turns, loops and one-ways, we got into a wider road and after a period, we again entered smaller streets and by-lanes. We reached Deepan's apartment about 8 PM. He had a covered parking space, a piece of luxury in urban living. We took the elevator up. Deepka greeted us at the door. She is a bright woman with a happy face. We sat down in the couch; the baby Vivan was in a crib on the side, playfully kicking legs. Vivan is a remarkably jolly baby; the happiness of a person is probably built in one's health. I played with the boy, the boy exhibited exuberant smiles.

Kirti was a well-read young man. He had read philosophy, literature and sciences. It was interesting to discuss with him about the views of life and observations by the philosophers. Was the universe an accident or did it have a design? Was there a designer? Was life statistical or is it predictable? We wandered in our thoughts and shared our experiences and observations. I appreciated his depth and insight. Deepan also participated; he had an engineering attitude. Life had to be lived, and not analyzed. Every moment was new and brought new experience. One had to be ready for the moment. I loved the thought process. I loved that they had their views. My views remained unclear, still evolving.

We sat down for a light supper. It was nice to be together with young people in supper. Deepka served and joined the table as the last person. It was late in the night for me. After supper, we talked a bit more. Deepan set up a mattress in the living room and my bed was done. I changed clothes and quickly went to sleep.

BOSTON

It was a bright Monday morning. We were up about 7 AM; the baby was still sleeping. Deepka gave me a cup of tea and three of us talked about family. I invited them to visit Boston, which they agreed. I also advised them to be in touch with others in the family. Deepka's parents lived in Chandigarh and they had their extended family around there. She would be visiting India in September for an extended stay. Deepka would go to drop them off and then go in December to bring them back.

Deepan's father had been hospitalized earlier in the year and he showed concern. I told him my gratitude to his mother for having been a good and caring daughter and wife. He liked her very much; they had strong bondage. We talked about their futures in the United Kingdom and the general plans. Deepan was not very much concerned. Since both are professionals, they hoped to be comfortable wherever they were.

I took a shower and got ready. Deepka had cooked food. Deepan got ready and we sat down for breakfast. Deepka also joined. It was nice for all to eat together. I enjoyed the company. Now it was time to go to the subway. I begged leave of Deepka. I touched her head and blessed. The baby was still sleeping; I went near his head and offered a silent blessing. Deepan and I walked to the subway station. It was about 10:30 in the morning. Deepan directed me to my train and he waited for a different train. I traveled to the airport.

Passing through the maze of pedestrian tunnels, stairways and checkpoints, I arrived at my gate for the flight. Virgin Atlantic staff seemed cordial. We boarded and took off in time. I was in Boston at local time 3:30 PM. The total duration of my trip was twenty-one days.

One feels more familiar and comfortable in Boston. I began helping a mother who wanted to find her way to the subway. Suddenly I was a host than a guest!

AFTERWORD

B ijoy Misra has given us a philosophical account of how a son struggles to come to terms with a father who gave his life not to the family but to the nation and community: a man who was born on this Spring day in the Nineteenth twenty in an India that was completely different from the country that we know now. I met Bijoy's wonderful father when the old hero visited Cambridge in the summer of Nineteen ninety-four on the occasion that he attended the Mahabharata Seminar which we held each week in the Sanskrit Department on Church Street. I vividly recall listening to the grand old gentleman perform some of his poetry and the melodic voice that he gave to it, drawn from centuries of song culture.

This remarkable book is about a son's return to his natal terrain and his attempt to understand and retrieve part of his father's life and values. It is the voice of a migrant who has crossed seas and continents in pursuit of not simply material ends but of scientific and intellectual possibility; a migrant who received his initial impulse in life from that paternal voice. So many threads are woven into this text and its gentle complexity is remarkably profound for we all know that the past dominates every second of our present existence but the problem is that we are unaware of its actual content and composition and of the lost nature of its grain; hence must make extra-ordinary efforts to perceive and understand what it is that has preceded this, our contemporary moment.

In their movement across time and space human beings relinquish not simply love of person but also love of place. In his book Bijoy has managed to retrace and recall those disconnections and the value systems which led to their genesis. He has described how it is that human beings join and divide, the grounds upon which they merge and separate and how our emotions are both created and diminished by such small irreversible details of experience. If we are made for love we are also unmade by its loss or absence, whether such love be spiritual, moral, political, artistic, or simple earthly affection.

Misra is a cartographer of such transformations, their vicissitudes and their minute and exacting metaphors; just as the acoustic in the universe informs how human beings speak and how birds and other animals sing, so our author has offered us a precisely modulated depiction of how his own mental and emotional inheritance came to be composed during childhood and youth inOrissa, and simultaneously by the greatness of the Indian cosmos and its ancient culture. This book is the story of that attempt at repossession and discovery.

In his book the author has catalogued this journey, a voyage towards the ancestral conditions which once so informed him, perhaps even from before he was born, and he has portrayed how it is to pursue such an inquiry, such an odyssey of recovery and comprehension. What is recorded within these pages is the universal effort to exist and to endure not simply in the present which we inhabit but simultaneously in the past—with its necessary compulsions—as well as in the future with all its ideals and aspiration.

What we accomplish in life possesses a moral force of some distinction and some degree; in this wonderful travelogue Misraji tells us how it has been for him to struggle, carefully and deliberately and sometimes only in retrospect, to refine that apprehension of our moral reception in the world: what we have received from the past and what we intend to convey towards those who inherit from us. I feel privileged to have shared this unique trajectory and its particularly fine remembrance of things past.

Kevin McGrath
Harvard University
March 20th, Two Thousand & Fourteen

EPILOGUE

I thank you my reader for making the journey with me. For various reasons, people move and do not get an opportunity to observe. Looking at our origin through a window is not always straightforward. While other visitors and journalists write about us, we do not make it convenient to write about ourselves. Mine was an effort to educate my children and encourage many other immigrants to observe and express. Sociology changes with culture and it is difficult to observe how a culture like India's might adopt to the new world. There is media invasion and confusion among people on the values and directions. India's colonial past is still a curse to her heritage; some parts are possibly permanently deformed. Philosophy has morphed to jingoism and survival, the beauty of analysis slowly getting lost. It is not clear if philosophy only breeds in prosperity, a hungry man has to eat first.

My expedition was to check if the sacrifice that my father had made yielded results. The principal product that I noticed that the Orissa state and Oriya language existed, though not as flowering as they should. The average person however was looking outside of the state than discovering its gems and history. The language education is weak leading to the trap of less creative work that the nineteenth century Englishmen had planned. I have not sampled other parts of the country, but Orissa has suffered.

What should we do? We write, think, speak and cultivate the culture. We dig to discover manuscripts and print. We marvel at the creativity of our people and engage ourselves in furthering the work. We do everything to help restore the dignity and heritage of our literature, customs, habits and culture. Each person has a role and each of us should join in the new revival process. We must succeed for the sake of the country, for the sake of the soil.

My friend Gokul Patnaik in Delhi was the first to encourage me to write. While I had the intention to create a dialog with my son, it became a travelogue through the persuasion of my friend Prasanna Hota in Delhi. Three readers Manas Behera, Tanuj Pradhan and SC Choudhury sent me compliments from unknown locations. Sri Choudhury helped me connect with Anupam Choudhury in Delhi who took time to read the manuscript. I am thankful to my friend Sudhanshu Misra in Boston who first suggested that I should compile the travel story into a book. My High School senior Mr. Devdas Chhotray in London and my father's friend Professor Manoj Das in Pondicherry, India sent me their gracious comments. I thank my friends Dr. Sajed Kamal and Dr. Kevin McGrath for sharing their written comments on the manuscript. I express my gratitude to all members of my family who have allowed their story to be told in the context of my travel. Nagendra Mallick and Laxmicharan Padhy helped me in arranging the schedule in travel in Orissa. Some of the living names have been altered; the facts and impressions are entirely as to my observation. I thank Dr Kanak Hota for the final proof-reading. I beg apology in advance for any errors or omissions.

I wrote the diary from recollections in the fall of 2012. My final revision was in December, 2016. Our friend Manilal Tripathy passed away December 1, 2012. My brother Sanjoy passed away January 19, 2015. My youngest aunt passed away in March, 2015. I dedicate this writing to their memory and all my friends whose association and wishes sustain me in the world.

Harvard University
Cambridge, MA
April 25, 2017.

Bijoy Misra was born at the dawn of India's independence in Cuttack, India. He was named 'Bijoy' which means victory in Sanskrit and Oriya. Impressed by his father's activism he engaged in public service whilst attending school.

Trained as a physicist he was honoured with medals and awards which brought him to the US as a Visiting Scientist in Nineteen seventy-two. He returned home to support his mother and family. The commotion and political instability in India during the Seventies made him leave India again to find a new residence at MIT. He has been involved in research and teaching at MIT and Harvard University since Nineteen Seventy-four. Besides professional and scientific work, Misra is active in community affairs, organizing service to immigrant Indians and their children. He is a Sanskrit scholar and has been involved with teaching and research in Sanskrit since Nineteen Ninety-two. He writes in Oriya and is the founder of South Asian Poets of New England which works to create a literary voice in the community; he has edited books for the Ramakrishna Vedanta Society of Boston, and has translated old Oriya texts for Oxford University Press. Lately, still following in his father's footsteps, he has been assisting inner-city students, developing the curriculum and teaching enrichment classes to help improve science learning. He currently explores his Indian heritage examining the cultural history of India through a project initiative entitled India Discovery Center, based in Lincoln, USA.

He lives with his wife in Lincoln, Mass., and has two children and three grandchildren.

www.ingramcontent.com/pod-product-compliance
Lightning Source LLC
Chambersburg PA
CBHW052017070526
44584CB00016B/1795